This book belongs to

_____

...a Proverbs 31 Woman
in Contemporary Times

THE
Proverbs
31 *woman*

IN CONTEMPORARY TIMES

**A PRACTICAL GUIDE
FOR EVERY WOMAN**

CAREER   FINANCE   LIFESTYLE   MINISTRY   FAMILY

ENO JERRY

To find out more, go to *www.enojerry.com*
email: enojerry@gmail.com or call +234 905 456 2617

Published and Printed in Nigeria by

 máxximo

www.maxximo.com
+234 814 293 2770

But a woman who
fears the LORD,
she shall be praised.

Contents

Introduction		7
Chapter 1:	Power	11
Chapter 2:	Respect	15
Chapter 3:	Wisdom	47
Chapter 4:	Early Bird	65
Chapter 5:	Gentleness	73
Chapter 6:	Grow	83
Chapter 7:	Integrity	91
Chapter 8:	Discernment	97
Chapter 9:	Proactive	107
Chapter 10:	Blessed	117
Chapter 11:	Gifted	127
Chapter 12:	Balance	139
Chapter 13:	Inspiration	151
Chapter 14:	Conclusion	155

Introduction

I have always wondered how anyone could have all the virtues and qualities as detailed in the book of Proverbs 31. The Proverbs 31 Woman was the prophesy of King Lemuel's mother to her son. She described this woman to her son, King Lemuel. She started by saying in Proverbs 31:10 (AMPC), "A capable, intelligent and virtuous woman – who can find her? She is far more precious than jewels and her value is far above rubies or pearls". This woman seems to have everything all under control; she's a great wife, mother, she manages her home, she owns businesses, she cooks, she sews and the list goes on. What she doesn't seem to do is get tired. For me it is exciting and challenging all at the same time because she embodies every single thing you will want to embody. I am not given to agree with the opinion that it is impossible to be this woman because the bible says in Luke 1:37 (AMP), "For with God nothing [is or ever] shall be impossible". It therefore means that you can be this woman the bible took time to describe. I believe that God is an intentional God. He doesn't say a thing without meaning it. So, for this woman to be described for us in the bible, I believe God is saying we can be like her if we become intentional. Since we serve an intentional God, as His children, we also ought to be intentional in our actions.

There is no other place in the bible that we see the description of anyone as detailed as the virtuous woman, and I believe it was included in the Bible to serve as a model for who we can become with the help of the Holy Spirit. When you read Proverbs 31:10-31, you see a woman who is so strong yet so humble. Our society most of the time portrays womanhood as weak, feeble, unintelligent, naïve about financial matters, vain, clueless, and the list goes on, but the bible describes exactly the opposite. This woman is an embodiment of inner strength, beauty and brains, responsible and accountable, dependable, supportive, excellent, understanding, wise, prudent, frugal, etcetera.

In 2019, I started an online journey with thousands of women called "The Proverbs 31 Woman Challenge". This book has been birthed as an aftermath of the challenge and it's coming from the place of intentionality and the place of prayers towards becoming the Proverbs 31 Woman. I believe that you are reading this book right now because you also desire to be this woman just like I and thousands of women had the same desire few months ago. I want to reassure you that you can become the Proverbs 31 Woman and even more. The bible tells us in 2 Timothy 3:16 (NLT), "All Scripture is inspired by God and is useful to teach us what is true and to make us realize what is wrong in our lives. It corrects us when we are wrong and teaches us to do what is right". So, in this journey of becoming more, we will be learning from this Woman what we should do, who we should become and what we shouldn't do in our journey as women in contemporary times.

This book is a practical guide with daily activities to help you become a Virtuous Woman. My advice is this: don't be in a hurry to finish reading the book, but take the activities seriously as well and do them daily until you get to the end. We have had so many testimonies already from the online version and I believe you are next to testify. I can also assure you that the things you learn from this challenge will improve your marriage or relationship and for the single ladies, it will get you prepared and ready for your future which starts now. Strap your seat belts as we journey together.

Let's do this together!!!

Chapter

01

CAREER

FINANCE

LIFESTYLE

MINISTRY

FAMILY

POWER

"Who can find a virtuous woman? For her
price is far above rubies"
(Proverbs 31:10, KJV)

ing Lemuel's mother starts her prophesy on the Proverbs 31 Woman by saying in Proverbs 31:10 (KJV), "Who can find a virtuous woman? For her price is far above rubies". The root word that births the word Virtuous is "Virtue". In the New Testament (Mark 5:25-30, KJV), a multitude was pushing over Jesus and there was a woman with an issue of blood for twelve years who said, "If only I may touch but his clothes, I shall be whole". As soon as she touched the hem of Jesus garment, immediately she received her healing. However, the bible says that Jesus knew within Himself that "virtue" had gone out of him. The word "virtue" used in this scripture is translated as power. Apparently, when Jesus was asking who touched him, he did so because he knew that power had gone out of him. The word "virtue" as used in Proverbs 31 is the same word Jesus used in the New Testament narrative, meaning 'power'.

The first secret of the Proverbs 31 Woman was that she was powerful. It wasn't that her voice was strong or that she looked strong and acted strong. It wasn't that she was authoritative; rather her secret came from her secret place. She knew where to generate power from and she knew it could only come from having a robust prayer life. She knew how to be strong in the place of prayer. This woman must have had a prayer altar. For the Proverbs 31 Woman to have been as effective and resourceful as she was, it means that she had a place where she generated power and strength for each day.

When others were sleeping, she was awake (Proverbs 31:15). I believe she wasn't just awake but as a New Testament believer, I believe most of the time she was awake, she was generating power in the place of prayer. The Proverbs 31 Woman in Contemporary times must have a robust prayer life and a prayer altar that burns with fire. There shouldn't be coals on your altar. For you to do well in business or career, you must have a place where you generate power. Your business will not just thrive by only branding. What will bring your customers isn't just branding. The bible says in Ecclesiastes 8:4a (KJV), "Where the word of a king is, there is power". She went about her business with power. People were attracted to her life because of the favour of God upon her life. To be a Proverbs 31 Woman in Contemporary times, you need the favour of God upon your life. When God's favour is upon you, your little efforts will produce great results. The favour of God takes away labour from your

> **The Proverbs 31 Woman in Contemporary times must have a robust prayer life and a prayer altar that burns with fire.**

life. No wonder the bible says in Proverbs 18:22 (NIV), "He who finds a wife finds what is good and receives favour from the Lord".

With this knowledge, there are two things we need to ask God to do in our lives. The first is to ask for power and the second is to ask for favour.

PRAYER FOCUS

- O Lord *make me a woman of power in the name of Jesus. Amen.*
- O Lord, *endow me with your power and favour for business, career, academics and ministry.*

Chapter

02

CAREER   FINANCE   LIFESTYLE   MINISTRY   FAMILY

Chapter Two

RESPECT

#CHALLENGE 1: *"Never spiteful,
she treats him generously all her life long"*
(Proverbs 31:12 MSG).

The Proverbs 31 Woman is described as **never** spiteful. The synonyms of the word 'spiteful' include malicious, mean, nasty, cruel, unkind, unfriendly, snide, hurtful, bitter, hostile, rancor, vicious, and hateful. The bible didn't just say she isn't spiteful but further adds that she treats him *generously all her life long*. I am sure that the Proverbs 31 Woman didn't marry a perfect man because there are no perfect men or women anywhere. What this invariably means is that despite his probably annoying or imperfect behaviour and actions, she never reacts back or gets bitter. She is always generous and kind to him. This may sound like a tough call for some people because of the personality and character of their husbands. But the bible didn't say she chooses when to be nice and when to be spiteful to her husband based on what he does or doesn't do; rather, it says she is generous towards him as long as she lives. Wow, that means the moment you get married to your husband, you are signing up for a lifetime of generosity and kindness and saying a total no to any kind or shade of spitefulness.

For those of us already married, we must learn how to overlook or ignore most of the things our husbands do to us or does in our marriage. Your response to me may be, what about him? Shouldn't he do likewise for me? Well this is my answer: the scripture we read, was speaking specifically to the woman and no mention was given of the man. The earlier you see and appreciate that marriage isn't a competition, neither is it about who does what first, but rather see marriage as a ministry, the easier it will be for you to handle issues that may arise in your marriage. Since the focus on this scripture is on women, we will stay within our context.

It's possible to have a conversation with your spouse about something he did that wasn't right, or that you didn't like, without being spiteful. It's very possible; however, our challenge most times is with the power we have given to our emotions. Our emotions most times dictate to us how to react and how not to react to the issues we face. At times, it's the people around us that advise us on how to deal with the issues or challenges we are facing in marriage and most often than not, their advice isn't usually based on what the bible admonishes. As a woman you must deliberately ask yourself this pertinent questions and answer them:

Who are you listening to?
Who is advising you?
Who are you talking to?
Who are you learning from?

The person you are listening to, talking to, learning from or getting advice from must be someone who knows what the Bible says about marriage and is a strong believer of the institute of marriage, God's own way. There are too many people counseling and advising couples on marriage but not too many people are deriving their standards from the bible. Our Christian values are gradually eroding for worldly standards and points of view.

As wives, one of the best ways of putting into practice this verse is to be quick to forgive and never in a hurry to revenge or pay back. The bible says in 1 Peter 3:9 (NLT), "Don't repay evil for evil. Don't retaliate with insults when people insult you. Instead, pay them back with a blessing. That is what God has called you to do, and he will bless you for it". Blessing instead of cursing, being generous with good compliments instead of vengeful isn't just for strangers but also towards our husbands. For every time you keep malice, ignore your spouse, refuse to make a meal for him, refuse to help him in ways you usually will do or say unkind words to him, especially because of something he did to you, bear in mind that you aren't fulfilling this scripture. The Proverbs 31 Woman in our contemporary times doesn't have to struggle to prove a point to her husband by treating him the same way he treats her. When you treat him the way Peter admonished in 1 Peter 3:9, God will bless you. It's no longer about him but about God.

Another scripture that will help you treat your spouse right is 1Peter 4:8 (NIV) which says, *"Above all, love each other deeply, because love covers a multitude of sins."* There is a deep kind of love that overlooks your spouse's wrongs. If you haven't started over looking what your husband does or does not do, you haven't started loving deeply. Successful relationship is not the absence of bad behavior but the overlooking of them. Most of the things we are spiteful about in our spouse are not destiny related. If it isn't destiny related, please shut your eyes. Like I always say, instead of nagging, worrying, complaining about the things he is isn't getting right, spend that time praying about it.

RESPECT

Most times, wives say they respect their husbands while husbands say their wives don't respect them. I remember the early years of marriage, too many times my husband complained that I didn't respect him and usually I will become so defensive because I believed I respected him. It took me a long while to understand and show him respect in the way he would understand and appreciate.

The bible says in Ephesians 5:33, "Let each one of you in particular so love his wife as himself, and let the wife see that she respects her husband". Notice, Paul didn't say respect your husband the way you see in the movies, or the way you see your neighbour respect her husband or the way your mum respects your father or the way your friends respect their husbands. He just said wives respect your husband. Men gravitate to the place where they receive honour and respect. The best side of your husband is revealed when you honour and respect him and the worst side of your husband is revealed when you disrespect or dishonor him. Honour is like sweet medicine; it is the strongest weapon any woman could ever have on a man.

Some Practical Ways Wives can honour their Husbands:
- Stop acting like you're his mother: Allow your husband make mistakes and learn from them, especially when he wants to do things his own way. Don't force him to do it your way. Don't scold him or speak to him like he is a child. Always remember, he is your husband not your son. My husband would admonish women by saying to them to stop trying to train their husbands; it's your children the bible asked that you train. Your role in his life is to make suggestions and don't make a fuss if he refuses to listen to you.

- Allow God to be the enforcer in your relationship: You can make your suggestion but always remember that it isn't your job to change him. It's God's job. Pray more for your husband and rely on God to change him.

- Honour the man you want him to be: Many times, we complain that he doesn't deserve to be honoured and respected and we keep using this quote, "respect is earned". I have heard a lot of testimonies of men who changed because their wives treated them better than they deserved after they had done something wrong. I encourage you, treat your husband better than he deserves and you will see a changed man. You speak destiny into him when you treat him that way. Men love honour and will become the best form and version of themselves in an atmosphere of respect and honour.

- Cover his faults and focus on his strengths: When relating with your husband please stop using the phrase, "I warned you" or "I told you" especially when he doesn't take your advice and things turn out badly. The devil most times wants us to focus more on the weaknesses of our spouse than their strengths. But God wants us to think on the good elements of our lives and relationships. The bible says in Phil 4:8 (MSG), "Summing it all up, friends, I'd say you'll do best by filling your minds and meditating on things true, noble, reputable, authentic, compelling, gracious- *the best, not the worst; the beautiful, not the ugly;* things to praise, not things to curse".

Finally, every man has a language of honour; so find out your husband's own language. Find out what you will do that will suggest that you respect him and what you currently do that suggests a lack of respect. Also ask him to tell you, and whatever he tells you, please resolve to do right and stick to it.

Word of Caution

- You can't treat your husband the same way your friend or neighbour treats her husband because most men interpret respect differently. Every man wants respect but what respect means to one man may vary from what it means to another.

- When asking him to tell you what respect means to him, be very sincere about it. Don't put pressure on your spouse for a response. He may want to think about your question and if so, please allow him think about it and get back to you. In the meantime, you can write out what you think respect means to him and later go through it with him.

- When asking, let him know that you want to be a better woman so you need his answer to help you treat him right.

GENEROSITY

The bible tells us that the Proverbs 31 Woman (Proverbs 31:12) treats him (her husband) generously all her life long.

The word "generous" means liberal, lavish, magnanimous, giving, bountiful, unselfish, free-handed, etcetera. Women, we have believed so much in the past decades that women are receivers while the men are the givers. So, a young girl gets into a relationship with the opposite sex and automatically expects him to provide almost everything she needs. In marriage, wives expect their husbands to meet all the demands of the home front and her own personal needs and no one imagines or thinks that the man would love if he also receives gifts and have his own needs met. However, the Proverbs 31 Woman shows us that as women we must be generous towards our husbands. Generosity can be both tangible and intangible. Tangible generosity is when you give physical gifts to your husband while intangible generosity ranges from compliments, good will, niceness, help, care, etcetera.

The Proverbs 31 Woman in contemporary times is that woman who supports her husband wherever he needs help. She doesn't mind using her own money to buy items for her home, she isn't selfish in her dealings with her husband, she isn't busy collecting and acquiring from the man without giving back in return. She goes out of her way to shop for him with her own money, meet his needs even as he meets hers; she understands that she isn't in a competition with him and willing to step in whenever the need arises.

> **the Proverbs 31 Woman shows us that as women we must be generous towards our husbands.**

This woman is generous in forgiving an insult or injury, and is free from petty resentfulness or vindictiveness. For instance, if her husband upsets her in the morning before he leaves for work, she deliberately refuses to stay upset towards him. Instead she makes his meal, goes all out to do something nice and kind for the man even though he had offended her; she sends him lovely messages during the day; she acts like she was never offended and prepares a meal and a warm bath for him to have as soon as he returns from work. I believe there isn't a man whose wife will treat him this way, so magnanimously that he wouldn't do almost anything for that woman except he is a son of Belial. As wives, most of our problems will be solved when we pay back evil behaviour with good behaviour.

Another interesting synonym of the word spiteful is "ill-natured" which means bad-tempered or mean-spirited. When someone is referred to as mean spirited, it means the person is wicked. There shouldn't be any trace of wickedness in us. No one should ever want to describe you and use the word "wicked". Peradventure we are referred to as being wicked, we need to repent today. Another synonym of the word spiteful is malicious which means intending to harm or upset someone. There were times in the past when I was upset with my husband for something, I felt he did to me and I would look for ways to payback with even a more painful action than what he did to me. Some of us have gone all out to harm our spouse because of a temporary situation. Nothing done in anger will ever produce a good outcome. The Proverbs 31 Woman knew how to discard wrong and negative emotions and instead exhibited good and positive emotions in her relationships. You must learn how to bridle your whole body; put your emotions under subjection and be the one in control of it.

Remember, the Bible says that this Proverbs 31 Woman is never spiteful all her life. Like I said earlier, I believe she didn't marry a perfect man but she is a woman who has learnt how to control her emotions. You must understand that your ability to control your emotions isn't necessarily for the benefit of your husband or the people around you even though they would benefit from it, but ultimately it is for your own good. You are the first beneficiary of a well-balanced emotion. It is necessary that you possess these virtues for your own sanity, well-being and peace of mind.

BROKENNESS

I believe that before a woman can successfully be all of these, she must be a woman that is vulnerable in the hands of God. The bible says in Psalms 51:16-17 (KJV), "For thou desirest not sacrifice; else would I give it: thou delightest not in burnt offering. The sacrifices of God are a broken spirit: a broken and a contrite heart, O God, thou wilt not despise". God desires that your spirit and mind is broken. This means that God is looking for a humble spirit. Most times as women, why we find it difficult to listen to our husbands is because of our egos. Just the same way men are egoistic, women are also egoistic.

- Brokenness is about your sensitivity, vulnerability and your ability to break down in God's presence.
- It is the shattering of self will. It is a place where God tames you.
- Brokenness is when God strips you of every self-reliance or self-dependence.
- Brokenness is the place where God is constantly against your flesh. If you are a broken woman, God will constantly fight every anger,

bitterness, jealousy, envy, wrath, deception, slander, gossip etcetera, in your life.

- Brokenness never cares about the environment or what people think. One of the awesome things about brokenness is that it says I might be bigger than someone, but I am willing to remain under that person. A Virtuous Woman must be a woman of humility.

Imagine God bringing you to a place where you don't have an opinion, when you don't care who wins in an argument or not. Your relationships are no longer about winning but more about what God is saying.

PRAYER FOCUS

- O Lord, *please help me forgive my husband, my fiancé, my dad, my brother, etcetera.*
- *Mend /fix my broken heart in the name of Jesus. Please teach me to trust once again in the name of Jesus.*
- O Lord, *my marriage must work. Every challenge I saw and experienced in my marriage in the past years, I will not see nor experience them moving forward.*
- *My marriage will be a safe haven for me and my children in the name of Jesus.*
- *Every battle I fought in the past, I will not fight again. Every new battle that wants to arise currently or in the future, I terminate you now in the name of Jesus. Amen!!!*

Further Reading and Meditation:

- Stop recalling past wrongs or hurts or bitterness in present day conversations with your spouse, fiancé or friends.

- Proverbs 10:12 (ESV), "Hatred stirs up strife, but love covers all offenses".
- Proverbs 19:11 (ESV), "Good sense makes one slow to anger, and it is his glory to overlook an offense".
- Ecclesiastes 7:21-22 (ESV), "Do not take to heart all the things that people say, lest you hear your servant cursing you. Your heart knows that many times you yourself have cursed others".
- Ephesians 4:2-3 (ESV), "With all humility and gentleness, with patience, bearing with one another in love, eager to maintain the unity of the Spirit in the bond of peace".

ACTIVITIES

DAY 1

#CHALLENGE 1: *"Never spiteful, she treats him generously all her life long" (Proverbs 31:12, MSG).*

ACTIVITY 1: Today you will speak well of your husband, fiancé, father, brothers or close male friends. Don't use any rude or cruel word in your communication. Make sure you aren't giving out a negative or nasty body language while communicating with him.

_____

_____

_____

_____

- During this challenge, married women please focus on your husband, while the singles or unmarried, will focus on their fiancé, father, brother or close male friends.

This is important because as Singles, the way you currently speak to your father, brothers or close male friends is a pointer to what your relationship will be like with your husband. If you do not have regard for them, that's the same attitude you will most likely take into your marriage.

ACTIVITY 2: Have a journal where you will record your progress each day or you can write below. Write out what your spouse did that should have annoyed you (if any) and how you dealt with it without reacting spitefully. At the end of each day, you can keep track of how you reacted, and note areas for improvement (if any).

_____

_____

_____

DAY 2

#CHALLENGE 1: *"Never spiteful, she treats him generously all her life long" (Proverbs 31:12, MSG).*

Good Day Virtuous Woman, today you will be reflecting on a few things.

ACTIVITY 1: Write out a list of all the things that your spouse/fiancé does to you that gets you upset and angry (if any).

_____

_____

_____

ACTIVITY 2: After you have listed them out, mention them one after the other and make a resolve that these things would not affect your marriage or relationship anymore.

Tips for Today:

Learn to ignore the things your spouse does to you. Ignore it. Live free of offence. If it isn't destiny related, let go.

Prayer Focus:

- Father, every distraction that has consistently affected my marriage/relationships negatively, today I command them to disappear in the name of Jesus.
- I shut my eyes to everything that irritated me in the past in my marriage/relationship in Jesus' name.

Keep Winning!!! You can do this!!!

THE PROVERBS 31 WOMAN IN CONTEMPORARY TIMES

DAY 3

#CHALLENGE 1: *"Never spiteful, she treats him generously all her life long" (Proverbs 31:12, MSG).*

Good Day Virtuous Woman, I just want to encourage you and tell you how amazing you are doing. We are making good progress. You are no longer the woman you used to be. So please don't give up. You can do this!!!

Today's Challenge is Exciting!!!

We are looking at the subject matter, RESPECT.

ACTIVITY 1:

1. What does Respect mean to you? How do you show respect to your husband?

    _____

    _____

    _____

2. What does respect mean to your husband? How does he expect you to respect him?

    _____

    _____

    _____

3. With the knowledge of the above, give examples of things you will do that will show you respect him and things if done will be viewed as disrespectful.

    _____

    _____

_____

_____

4. Make up your mind to respect him the way he likes/wants it.

Show your spouse honour today!!!

Prayer Focus:
O Lord, help me to be respectful to my husband in Jesus' name. Help me understand respect from his perspective and not mine in Jesus' name. Help me to be deliberate in submitting to my husband in Jesus' name, Amen.

For Singles: O Lord, help me to be respectful towards my dad and older brothers in Jesus' name.
- Teach me what it means to submit to a man even before I get married in Jesus' name.
- O Lord, may my future spouse never complain that I am disrespectful in Jesus' name. Amen!!!

DAY 4

#CHALLENGE 1: *"Never spiteful, she treats him generously all her life long" (Proverbs 31:12, MSG).*

ACTIVITY 1: Be generous to your husband /fiancé today. You can buy him a gift, take him out or just show little acts of kindness which you normally wouldn't have done. You may not need to spend money, just in case you aren't financially buoyant at the moment. Don't feel compelled to spend money. There are generous actions you can take today.

You can also choose to be generous with your praise especially for women who do not praise their husband. Make him feel like the king (he is). You can call him beautiful names that will make him feel like he's walking on the moon.

ACTIVITY 1: Act on your ideas today. You have a full day to do several things that should be all about him. It doesn't have to be his birthday before you act nicely or get him a gift or take him out for a dinner.

ACTIVITY 2: Write out ways you are going to show generosity towards your spouse. Write out what you will be doing to show little acts of kindness.

_____

_____

_____

Prayer Focus:
- Lord, as I show my husband generosity today, may he respond favorably towards me.
- O Lord, let the seeds I sow today bring me closer to my spouse and bring us closer to each other in Jesus' name, Amen.

DAY 5

#CHALLENGE 1: *"Never spiteful, she treats him generously all her life long"* (Proverbs 31:12, MSG).

Good Day Virtuous Woman, I am super excited at what God is set to do in your life and I encourage you to believe God for the best results whilst we are on this challenge. The bible says in Habakkuk

2:3 (NKJV), "For the vision is yet for an appointed time, but at the end it shall speak, and not lie: though it tarries, wait for it; because it will surely come, it will not delay." Your earnest desires for your marriage will come to pass. I see God rewarding all the seeds you are deliberately sowing whilst in this challenge with a mighty great harvest.

The Bible says in Genesis 8:22 (ESV), "While the earth remains, seedtime and harvest, cold and heat, summer and winter, day and night, shall not cease." The seeds you are sowing each day by carrying out the different activities will bear fruit.

ACTIVITY 1: Thank God for the gift of the best husband ever (even if you don't feel like it; confess it), best dad and best brothers ever. What you confess will become your reality in a matter of time.

_____

_____

_____

ACTIVITY 2: For every time you see your husband today, give him a warm and captivating smile. The bible says that a merry heart doeth good like a medicine: but a broken spirit drieth the bones (Proverbs 17:22, KJV). It may not make sense to you, especially if your spouse got you upset, however that's even why you must respond with a smile. I know you can do this. Smile!!!

DAY 6

#CHALLENGE 1: *"Never spiteful, she treats him generously all her life long" (Proverbs 31:12, MSG).*

Good Day Virtuous Woman, today you will be praying for your husband and for those unmarried you will be praying for your future husband.

ACTIVITY 1: You will spend one hour in prayers for your husband. I know you have a busy schedule but please make out time and pray for him. He needs your prayers. This is important as the bible says in James 5:16 (NLT) "Confess your sins to each other and pray for each other so that you may be healed. The earnest prayer of a righteous person has great power and produces wonderful results".

Our focus from the scripture above is that the earnest prayer of a righteous person has great power and produces wonderful results. As you pray for your husband or future husband, your prayers will produce wonderful testimonies in Jesus name. Below are a few prayer points to guide you but it isn't exhaustive.

Prayer Focus:
1. My husband will not die but shall live to declare the works of the Lord in the land of the living.
2. My husband must serve God all the days of his life. O Lord, grow my husband's passion and commitment to the things of God.
3. O Lord, grant me the grace to love my husband more as each day unfolds in Jesus name.

4. Every weakness or negative habit in the life of my husband, (mention his name and the weakness) today, I command them to die.

5. Today, I decree, may his areas of weakness become areas of strength in the name of Jesus.

6. O Lord, please bless my husband. Prosper the works of his hands. Give him resounding testimonies in Jesus' name.

7. For the unbelieving husband: O Lord, may my husband have a personal encounter with you today. Save his soul. Let him give his life to Christ.

For the unmarried PRAY:

1. O Lord bless me with a good man; bless me Lord with a man that fears God.

2. O Lord, bless me with a man that will love me.

3. Today, I decree, no more heart breaks. No more meeting of the wrong kind of men. My paths shine brighter and brighter.

4. Today, I decree, I will not marry a wicked man, a woman chaser, a woman beater, or a stingy man in the name of Jesus.

5. O Lord, cause me to be sensitive in the day of my visitation. When the good man comes, help me to recognize him.

6. O Lord, make me a good woman; make me to be a Virtuous Woman that my husband and children will praise and bless me in Jesus name.

Amen!!!

DAY 7

#CHALLENGE 1: *"Never spiteful, she treats him generously all her life long"* (Proverbs 31:12, MSG).

Good Day Virtuous Woman. Like I said earlier, this woman did not marry a perfect man because there are no perfect men just the same way that there are no perfect women. So even when he offended her or acted in a way that she didn't like, she never retaliated. She was a woman who was in control of her emotions. She didn't allow her emotions control her.

Most times we become rude, cruel, disrespectful or bitter when our spouse hurts or offends us. But the Bible says all the days of her life she treats him generously and she is "never" spiteful. 'Never' means at no time in the past or future is she spiteful. God really needs to help some of us. Today, you will be deliberately praying to God concerning your emotions.

ACTIVITY 1: Spend time praying for your emotions today. Don't be in a hurry to stop. 1 Peter 5:8, the devil goes about like a roaring lion, seeking whom (whose marriage, peace, Joy, etcetera) to devour. Don't give him a place in your home. Shut the door on his face by PRAYING.

Prayer Focus:
1. Today, I take control of my emotions. I put you under subjection. You will not control me in Jesus name. I am in charge/control over my emotions in the name of Jesus.

2. O Lord, help me. I have no power of my own. I can't do these things based on my human strength. Lord, release your strength in my life in the name of Jesus.
3. Every battle I fought in my marriage in the past, I will not fight them again. I command you battles to disappear now.
4. My marriage, hear the word of the Lord, you will be a source of inspiration to other marriages in the name of Jesus.
5. I decree peace, joy, love, self-control, forgiveness, patience, goodness in my home, my marriage, and my relationships.
6. Every power that says I will not be happily married, today I shut you up in the name of Jesus. Every power that says I will not stay married, today I shut you up in Jesus name.

Declare After Me: I must stay in control of my emotions in Jesus Name.

ACTIVITY 2: If you can speak in the Holy Ghost, begin to speak in the Holy Ghost NOW.
I decree and declare over you in the name of Jesus, you have a good marriage. I decree, your marriage must work. I decree, it will be a heaven on earth experience in the name of Jesus. I decree that your home will be filled with joy, peace, love, happiness, laughter in the name of Jesus.

For the unmarried ladies, whatsoever you desire to see in your husband call it forth, declare and confess it. In a short while, it will become your reality if you do not faint in Jesus' name. Galatians 6:9

(KJV), "And let us not be weary in well doing: for in due season we shall reap, if we faint not".

DAY 8

#CHALLENGE 1: *"Never spiteful, she treats him generously all her life long" (Proverbs 31:12, MSG).*

Good Day Virtuous Woman. Today is a day for reflection.

ACTIVITY 1: Write a list of all the good things you know about your husband. (E.g. what are those attributes that attracted you to him? What made you marry him?).
For those engaged, why do you want to marry your fiancé?

_____

_____

_____

ACTIVITY 2: Write a list of all the things that he does that gets you upset or that you do not like.

_____

_____

_____

ACTIVITY 3: Weigh the two lists opposite each other, which one is more?
- Focus on the list that has the things that you like about him. Whatsoever you focus on, will grow. Whenever he offends you, always remember the positive list (things) above the offense.
- Then pray about the areas you don't like and make a resolve that you will no longer complain or nag about them. Rather than nag, just keep praying until you see him change in those areas.

The only areas that should give you concern is if the areas he is doing wrong are destiny related. It then means you need to pray more and trust God for a change. However, if it isn't destiny related, please learn to overlook it.

Note: This exercise may take the whole day. The more you reflect throughout the day, the more likely you will remember nice things you have forgotten about your spouse. Wherever you go today, take your journal with you and put down whatever you remember. You may be shocked at how much you have forgotten.

DAY 9

#CHALLENGE 1: *"Never spiteful, she treats him generously all her life long" (Proverbs 31:12, MSG).*

Good Day Virtuous Woman. Today, we will be focusing on forgiveness and the need to forgive.

What is Forgiveness?
- To forgive is to let go.
- To forgive is to be the bigger person in a relationship.
- To forgive could be giving up your rights of being right just for peace.
- To forgive is to be free.
- To forgive is to live in good health.
- To forgive means you think about the person and the offense and you don't feel any form of hurt/pain or anger.
- To forgive means to be in control of your emotions.
- To forgive means to surrender your hurt and pain to God.
- To forgive is to rely on God's strength and grace.

We all need to learn how to forgive and let go of past hurt, pain and offense. The bible says in Colossians 3:13 (NIV), "Bear with each other and forgive one another if any of you has a grievance against someone. Forgive as the Lord forgave you".

You may be the one that needs to ask your spouse or fiancé for forgiveness or someone needs your forgiveness or someone may need your forgiveness in the future.

ACTIVITY 1: If you are the offender: Ask your husband or fiancé for forgiveness, for wrongs of the recent past if any. If you are a single lady and you aren't talking to your dad, it's time to make peace with him.

ACTIVITY 2: If you are the one that was offended: If your husband offended you, hurt you or betrayed you, it's time to forgive and let go. You can't keep holding that grudge or hurt. It isn't good for your health and well-being.

ACTIVITY 3: Send text messages to anyone (if any) that you need to forgive and mean it stating that you have forgiven them. This is necessary especially if they already know that you are unhappy with them because of an offense.

The bible says in Romans 12:18 (NIV), "If it possible, as far as it depends on you, live at peace with everyone".

DAY 10

#CHALLENGE 1: *"Never spiteful, she treats him generously all her life long" (Proverbs 31:12, MSG).*

SELF ASSESSMENT

1. How has these past 10 days been in your journey towards becoming the Proverbs 31 Woman?
2. How has your character/personality been shaped in these past days?
3. What have you learnt to do differently?
4. What new things have you learnt about your spouse/fiancé?
5. What new ways can you spice your marriage?

DAY 11

#CHALLENGE 1: *"Never spiteful, she treats him generously all her life long" (Proverbs 31:12, MSG).*

Good Day Virtuous Woman. Today, you will be fasting and praying for your spouse. You will fast from 6am till 2pm. Please take this seriously. You need to invest the seed of prayers into your husband's life and all that he does.

According to Matthew 7:21, "But this kind does not go out except by prayer and fasting." There are some stubborn challenges you may be facing in your marriage/relationship, and you have complained enough, but it's time to go to war in the spirit.

Prayer Focus:

1. O Lord, as my husband or fiancé goes out to indulge in sin/negative habits/addictions, may he have a personal encounter with you.

2. O Lord, I pray for the salvation of my spouse, my dad, brothers and close male friends.

3. Every power of addiction, I command it to break by fire in the name of Jesus.

4. O Lord, today I break every negative pattern in the life of my husband that is preventing him from fulfilling destiny in the name of Jesus.

5. Today, I break any relationship that diminishes or reduces his destiny. I cut them off in the name of Jesus.

6. Every relationship that takes his strength or distracts him, today I break such relationships in the name of Jesus

7. O Lord, bring the right kind of relationships into my husband's life; give him good men; raise destiny helpers for him in the name of Jesus.

For those not married, add this to your prayers:

O Lord, if they are wrong relationships my fiancé or future husband is in right now, I command them to break now. Whether they are relationships with the opposite sex or peers that are destiny destructive, I command such relationships to terminate now in the name of Jesus.

Declare after Me: My husband/ fiancé will never be found in the wrong place at the wrong time. He will not be in a destiny destructive relationship in the name of Jesus. Every scale over his eyes disappears right now in the name of Jesus.

DAY 12

#CHALLENGE 1: *"Never spiteful, she treats him generously all her life long" (Proverbs 31:12, MSG).*

ACTIVITY 1: You will be x-raying your life under the Word of God and if in any way you have acted or are acting in an ill-natured or malicious way towards your husband or fiancé, you will repent today.

ACTIVITY 2: Don't just say you will stop acting maliciously or stop being ill-natured; rather mean it. Be deliberate about staying in control of your emotions. Find out what sparks off or triggers these negative emotions in you and come up with positive ways of handling them.

Prayer Focus

1. O Lord, make me see and understand that I am the first beneficiary when my emotions are under control. Today, I take charge of my emotions.
2. Everything that causes me to act maliciously or ill-tempered today, I put you under control in the name of Jesus.
3. O Lord, I receive a gentle and quiet spirit in the name of Jesus.

Amen!!!

DAY 13

#CHALLENGE 1: *"Never spiteful, she treats him generously all her life long" (Proverbs 31:12, MSG).*

Good Day Virtuous Woman. Today's challenge is called, the 'I Love You Challenge'. You are going to be expressing your love to him. It sounds normal right? Well this time you won't just say I love you but you will show it.

ACTIVITY 1: What new ways can you show your husband how much you love him? Write them below and get to work.

_____

_____

_____

_____

Ideas to explore:
- You can design a card with the words on it and give it to him
- Allow him to have the last say over that matter
- Don't frown when next you do not agree with what he is saying
- Take him out on a date night
- Stop nagging and complaining
- Don't get angry and raise your voice at him
- Don't walk out on him while he is still talking to you
- Don't make ugly faces at him

You can add to the list ....

DAY 14

#CHALLENGE 1: *"Never spiteful, she treats him generously all her life long" (Proverbs 31:12, MSG)*.

Good Day Virtuous Woman, I looked up Proverbs 31:12 in a few other translations and each of the translations are such a blessing. Let's read them together.

"She helps him and never harms him all the days of her life" (God's Word Translation).

"She is good to him every day of her life" (Contemporary English Version). The word "good" means that which is morally right. Other synonyms of the word good are, gain, enjoyment, satisfaction, comfort, welfare.

Our focus today will be on the words: enjoyment and satisfaction.

ACTIVITY 1: **(For Married Women)** Today, deliberately bring satisfaction and enjoyment to your husband. We will examine satisfaction from the place of sex. A little bird told me that many married women use "sex" as weapons on their husbands. It's either they give the excuse of being tired after taking care of the children, or that they are angry with their husband or that they don't like sex, and the list continues. Whatever the reasons are, if you are anywhere close to what I have described, make a resolve today that you would not deny him the satisfaction of sex.
For the unmarried, today's challenge isn't for you. However, I need you to also make a resolve that when you get married in the near future (can someone say an Amen), you wouldn't deny your husband of sex or satisfaction.

DAY 15

#CHALLENGE 1: *"Never spiteful, she treats him generously all her life long" (Proverbs 31:12, MSG).*

Good Day Virtuous Woman, our scripture focus from God's Word Translation says, "She helps him and never harms him all the days of her life".

Today's challenge is on "HELP".

ACTIVITY 1: Today you are going to be "helping" your husband or fiancé.
You may know the areas he needs help however, if you don't know, ask him to tell you in what areas he would love you to help him.

Few ways you can help your spouse today:
1. Be more understanding and less demanding.
2. Help him through his weaknesses.
3. Pray for him.
4. Care for him.
5. Help him by not nagging and complaining.
6. Help him by supporting his visions and dreams.
7. Help him by coming up with initiatives and ideas.
8. Help him by offering financial support. There's nothing wrong if you cook the next meal, buy fuel/diesel, take him out for lunch or dinner, with your own money.

9. Help him by being a shoulder he can lean on and unburden. Don't get too busy to the extent that you stop being sensitive to his feelings.

The list is inexhaustible. The challenge is to make sure that today all you do is to find ways to help him.

Virtuous Woman, let us pray:
1. O Lord, please make these little changes I have begun to experience in my home and marriage permanent in my life.
2. O Lord, everything that says I will take three steps forward and ten backwards in my character, in my marriage, in my relationships, today I destroy it.
3. O Lord, my progress as a Virtuous Woman will be consistent and intentional in the name of Jesus.
4. Father, help me not to get tired on the way. Every voice of discouragement, voice of disappointment and regrets, voice of setback and failure, voice of depression, voice of worry and anxiety speaking to me, today I silence you by fire in the name of Jesus.
5. I decree, I will not be stopped in the name of Jesus. I cannot be stopped in the name of Jesus. I must complete this destiny journey in the name of Jesus. I can do this challenge in the name of Jesus. Amen!!!

Decree After Me: I am Unstoppable. My Marriage is Unstoppable. I cannot be stopped in the name of Jesus.

Chapter

03

CAREER

FINANCE

LIFESTYLE

MINISTRY

FAMILY

Chapter Three

WISDOM

#CHALLENGE 2: *"When she speaks, she has something*
worthwhile to say, and she always says it kindly"
(Proverbs 31:26 MSG).

I really love how the Proverbs 31 Woman reassures us to believe the scripture that says nothing is impossible with God once we believe. She makes this scripture come alive, "If you can believe, all things are possible to him who believes." (Mark 9:23, NKJV). It takes a woman of faith and courage to accept, believe and work towards becoming a Proverbs 31 Woman.

Other character traits we glean from the Proverbs 31 Woman is that when she opens her mouth to speak, she speaks wisdom. It therefore means that this woman is knowledgeable. She is constantly reading and growing in knowledge. Kindness is the grace of her lips. She is wise, intelligent and highly-cultured in her mind and in manners. She is graceful and even-tempered in all her ways. She isn't lord over her husband, tyrant over her servants and haughty towards her neighbours. She is an excellent example of one who has a meek and quiet spirit. Wow! What a wonder! Isn't she super amazing?

No wonder Apostle Peter admonishes us in 1 Peter 3 that we are to learn and emulate the women of old using Sarah as our role model. He admonishes wives to be meek and possess a quiet spirit. What this means is that amidst life's drama, problems, or bad behaviours from our husbands, we should maintain our composure. Don't react the way the devil will want you to react. Shock the devil by being extremely composed and in control of the situation. Be careful of the words that you speak especially when you feel upset. Our words are so powerful, and we can't retrieve them once they proceed out of our mouth.

I had a recent experience in my marriage, on a matter where I didn't agree with my husband's point of view. I believed more in my point of view and when he got upset, I wasn't bothered much because I really felt I was right this time around. While I prayed the next day, I heard God clearly tell me that He didn't want me to get upset or angry at my husband again. In fact, God told me what to do when my husband is upset. God said, (paraphrased) "when your husband is upset, don't get upset at the same time even if you think you have the right to be upset. When you get upset you escalate things and create a deeper misunderstanding. Your role is to ensure and maintain peace by saying and acting in a way that will calm him down." I believe this will help another woman, like the bible will say in Ecclesiastes 3, there's a time and a season for everything. You must be sensitive and discerning to know when to speak or when not to speak.

Even when you are right, you don't have to prove that you are right immediately especially if you sense tension around you and your spouse. Two upset people can never make a right. One person must let go and keep calm at that moment. So, for me, God told me that I can talk to my husband about that same issue on another day or time. Truth be told, another day or time may not be soon. This is where many of us make the mistake; we feel the need to talk about an issue immediately or the next day, but it could get into weeks later or months after the incident depending on the situation and the disposition of your spouse. Sometimes, you may never get to talk about the issue because time would have handled the issue or healed you. The bible says that Abigail told her husband Nabal (1 Samuel 25) when he was sober about what tragedy and disaster was going to befall them because of her husband's response to David, and not while he was drunk with alcohol. As wives, our husband's may not have had alcohol, but they all have their moments. This kind of discussions for best results, target your husband's sober moment. Our role is to be that bridge that ensures that there is peace in our homes and marriages.

Our role is to be that bridge that ensure that there is peace in our homes and marriages.

No wonder 1 Peter 3:5 (NKJV) says, "For in this manner, in former times, the holy women who trusted in God also adorned themselves, being submissive to their own husbands". As mentioned in this verse, the main reason why we can act gently and quietly is because like the women of old our trust is in God. We trust God to handle the situation and work it out for our good. We allow God to oversee the hearts of our husbands to understand our point of view instead of fighting and nagging. We trust God to handle the issues of addictions and bad behavior in the lives of our husbands.

The bible says in James 1:19 (KJV), "Wherefore, my beloved brethren, let every man be swift to hear, slow to speak, slow to wrath". Guard every word that comes out of your mouth preciously. The Proverbs 31 Woman wasn't given to too many words. The bible says in Proverbs 10:19 (KJV), "In the multitude of words sin is not lacking, but he who restrains his lips is wise". The Proverbs 31 Woman is that woman who goes for a board or management meeting and everyone keeps quiet, eager to hear what she has to say because her words are always full of wisdom and free of slander.

According to Proverbs 31:26 the bible says when she speaks she has something worthwhile to say. The synonyms of the word "worthwhile" are of value, beneficial, gainful, useful, advantageous, positive, profitable, significant and meaningful. Her speech helps and cheers the listeners. Her words are encouraging and educative. When people listen to her, they learn a thing or two. No idle word proceeds out of her mouth. If the Proverbs 31 woman was to be talked about or written about in today's times, we would have read that she is too busy for gossip on social media platforms, in the salons, at home or at work. As virtuous women, we need to give no time to idle chatter, gossip and unproductive watching of Television and social media.

KINDNESS

I have come to realize that if you aren't conscious of your actions and lifestyle, the society may make you to start acting unkindly or speaking unkindly towards others. Each day I step out or drive through my city, I see people abusing others and most of the time being plain obnoxious towards one another. It's easier to meet people who will respond to you unkindly than kindly these days. Even when they are in error, rather than acknowledge it, they will respond unkindly to you. We need to be deliberate about being kind and acting kind. You can't speak kindly to someone if you aren't a kind person or possess kindness as a quality. We need to become gentle, affectionate and more caring in our dealings with others and not just in our dealings with selected people.

The Proverbs 31 Woman isn't a woman that acts on impulse but rather a woman who has learnt the act of discipline. The bible says that even when she has a contribution or an opinion to share, she always says it kindly. The word "always" means it's not just a random act, but it's been translated to a lifestyle. Let's just say a word or prayer right now, "O Lord, help me become the woman I am reading about in Jesus name, Amen."

We need to become gentle, affectionate and more caring in our dealings with others...

According to Ephesians 4:29 (NLT), "Don't use foul or abusive language. Let everything you say be good and helpful, so that your words will be an encouragement to those who hear them". The bible doesn't give us permission at any time to use words that will hurt others rather every time we speak, our words should strengthen and encourage those listening. This includes those who will offend or who have offended you. You are supposed to reply them nicely and mean every word you say. It's a tough call, but you can do it.

How to maintain a calm disposition

The bible says in 1 Peter 3:4-5A (NLT) "You should clothe yourselves instead with the beauty that comes from within, the unfading beauty of a gentle and quiet spirit, which is so precious to God. This is how the holy women of old made themselves beautiful".

The Proverbs 31 Woman is a woman that understands that she should be more concerned about her inward disposition and make more investments inwardly than outwardly. She needs to possess a gentle and quiet spirit amidst a chaotic environment. It is important that we learn how to be calm, how to stay calm, how to meditate, ponder on the word of God and act strictly based on the leading of the Holy Spirit. So even when your environment is noisy, you are calm inwardly. She never allows the outward control her inward. She never allows her circumstances, challenges, or situations tamper with the peace and calmness she experiences within. How are you gaining control and staying in control of your emotions?

- One sure way of maintaining a calm disposition is by praying. You must build a wall of prayer fire around you. Use the nights to generate fire around your life; use the night to settle stubborn issues and challenges and face the day with a smile on your face. Your nights should be your time to **war** in prayers and your day time should be for maintaining **peace**.

If you are struggling with a riotous spirit, prayerfully ask God for a quiet and gentle spirit. A riotous spirit is when your mind keeps wandering during your time of prayer. When you spend a lot of your prayer time or some of your prayer time worrying about what you haven't done, the clothes that need ironing, the windows that you didn't close, the food to cook, the market you need to go to, the list you haven't written, a conversation you had during the day, someone that offended you, etcetera.

- Pray in the Holy Ghost to the point where you pray without getting distracted. One of the ways to achieve this is to always make sure your phone is on silent and far from you or switched off while you pray.
- Discipline your mind to stay focused while praying and not wandering.
- Don't be quick to react. Always think before you speak. You can sleep over that issue bothering you for some days until you know you can comfortably discuss the issue without getting upset or reacting negatively.
- You must be in control of your emotions. Your emotions don't dictate to you what you should do. Your emotions are poor decision makers so don't rely on them for solutions. You are first and foremost a spirit and your emotions are housed in your soul. Grow your spirit man to the level where it begins to dictate to your emotions what it should do.
- Don't speak when you are upset. Quote scriptures. Think on good thoughts.

FURTHER STUDY

- **Philip 4:8 (MSG),** *"Summing it all up, friends, I'd say you'll do best by filling your minds and meditating on things true, noble, reputable, authentic, compelling, gracious—the best, not the*

FURTHER STUDY

worst; the beautiful, not the ugly; things to praise, not things to curse".

- **Proverbs 17:27 (RSV)**, *"He who restrains his words has knowledge, and he who has a cool spirit is a man of understanding".*
- **Job 13:5 (NKJV)**, *"O that you would be completely silent, and that it would become your wisdom".*
- **Proverbs 21:23 (NASB)**, *"He who guards his mouth and his tongue, guards his soul from troubles".*
- **Proverbs 29:20 (ESV)**, *"Do you see a man who is hasty in his words? There is more hope for a fool than for him".*

ACTIVITIES

DAY 1

#CHALLENGE 2: *"When she speaks, she has something worthwhile to say, and she always says it kindly" (Proverbs 31:26, MSG).*

ACTIVITY 1: Today, you aren't expected to abuse or use harsh words on anyone. Don't even crack jokes that are offensive to your listeners. You are not permitted to use words like foolish, stupid, idiot and the list goes on, on anyone around you, not on your domestic staff, children, husband, friend, neighbours and even strangers on the road, which includes when driving your car.

Let's Go!!!

DAY 2

#CHALLENGE 2: *"When she speaks, she has something worthwhile to say, and she always says it kindly" (Proverbs 31:26, MSG).*

Let your words be few today. You don't need to be part of every conversation going on around you.

_____

_____

_____

- Listen more than you speak. James 1:19 (CEV) says, "My dear friends, you should be quick to listen and slow to speak or to get angry".

- Speak only when you have something *worthwhile* to say. If your contribution will not add valuable contribution to what has been said, remain quiet. Even Proverbs 17:28 (NLT) says, "Even fools are thought wise when they keep silent; with their mouths shut, they seem intelligent."
- Be abreast with what is happening around you, for instance, in politics, business, fashion, work and career. When we are knowledgeable, we can contribute meaningfully to conversations. Some of us need to go and study; start reading a book and listen to the news today. It is not too late to start.

ACTIVITY 2: Don't react angrily in all you do today and don't lash out at anybody. Don't quarrel with anyone today. Maintain a calm disposition.

ACTIVITY 3: Today you will be guarding your heart through your confessions. Proverbs 4:23 (NIV), "Above all else, guard your heart, for everything you do flows from it". List the things you will be guarding your heart from (e.g. Jealousy, anger, bitterness, envy, lies):

_____

_____

_____

_____

DAY 3

#CHALLENGE 2: *"When she speaks, she has something worthwhile to say, and she always says it kindly" (Proverbs 31:26, MSG).*

Good day Virtuous Woman, the second part of our Focal Scripture says, "and she always says it kindly". For every time this woman gives an instruction or a contribution, she always says it warmly, kindly, and compassionately without hurting people's self-esteem or self-worth. She is sensitive to the feelings of those around her and tries not to hurt or harm them. Some of us need to become more aware of the people around us and stop having expectations on how we expect them to behave. Treat them the way you would want to be treated and address them the way you would love to be addressed.

Some of us have lost destiny relationships because we didn't treat the people God brought into our lives kindly or warmly. Some of us have lost good nannies, and other domestic staff because of bad attitudes and verbal abuse. However, on our journey to becoming Proverbs 31 Women, we need to work on our personalities and characters. We need to become women who apply wisdom in their relationships and know how to strengthen profitable relationships.

Today we will be correcting all those around us in love.

ACTIVITY 1: Correct those around you, especially those living in your home in love. This includes your children, husband, siblings, domestic staff or nannies, in-laws, relations, colleagues and so on.

- Write out ways you can communicate effectively without being harsh or unkind.

_____

_____

_____

ACTIVITY 2: Don't give a response to everything that happens around you. Overlook most of them.

- At the end of the day, write out all the things you overlooked during the day.

_____

_____

_____

- If you were able to successfully overlook all the things you listed above, I assure you, with daily practice for the next two months, you would have successfully learnt how to manage your emotions.

DAY 4

#CHALLENGE 2: *"When she speaks, she has something worthwhile to say, and she always says it kindly" (Proverbs 31:26, MSG).*

Good day Virtuous Woman. From the English Standard Version, the scriptures in Proverbs 31:26 says, "She opens her mouth with wisdom, and the teaching of kindness is on her tongue". The word "wisdom" refers to discernment and most often than not, we lack discernment in our dealings with people. Most times, we don't even know what goes on in our home, work place, business, in the lives of our children, or husband. We are completely oblivious. For today's challenge, we will pray for wisdom.

ACTIVITY 1:Pray for Wisdom

1. O Lord, I ask for the wisdom of God today in all the conversations that I have and all the decisions I need to make. Please fill me with your Holy Spirit, which is the Spirit of Wisdom.

2. O Lord, the Bible says that wisdom is profitable to direct and in all my getting, I should get understanding. Today, I ask that the wisdom of God will direct all I do today. I pray that it will expose every hidden thing or everything I have been blind to; may my eyes be opened in Jesus' name.

3. O Lord, please help me to avoid taking rash decisions; rather, cause my decisions to be guided by good judgment.

4. O Lord, please give me the kind of wisdom you gave King Solomon to judge between right from wrong in Jesus' name.

5. Anybody that has been deceiving me, today let their plans be exposed in the name of Jesus.

Amen! Amen! Amen!

DAY 5

#CHALLENGE 2: *"When she speaks, she has something worthwhile to say, and she always says it kindly" (Proverbs 31:26, MSG).*

Good day Virtuous Woman. There is more to life than just getting married or being married. Your happiness and personal fulfillment cannot be hinged completely on the fact that you are married. You may think you will be fulfilled by just getting married but that is not where fulfillment comes from. If you are in doubt, ask those that are married. There's much more to life than walking down the aisle and

THE PROVERBS 31 WOMAN IN CONTEMPORARY TIMES

being married to a prince charming. Who you are, who you are becoming and your personal development are very important ingredients to being fulfilled in life. So, it's important that you begin to improve yourself. To achieve this, you may need to improve your vocabulary, read lots of books, stay updated on current affairs around your environment, improve your skills, learn a new skill, go on trainings, and generally keep growing.

One of the synonyms of the word "wisdom" is intelligence. Intelligence is the ability to acquire and apply knowledge and skills. So, there's the place of "acquiring" knowledge and the place of "applying" what we have acquired. You can only give what you have. You can only speak wisely and act kindly like the Proverbs 31 Woman, as a result of who you have become. If you don't have it, you can't give it.

ACTIVITY 1: Answer these questions:
• How many motivational/inspiring/educative books have you read or plan to read this year? Which books are you currently reading?
• How did you improve yourself last year? What are your plans/goals for this year on personal development? Which of them have you started implementing?

ACTIVITY 2: Start reading motivational or educative books today (especially for those who aren't reading or haven't read any yet).

ACTIVITY 3: Draw up a plan of where you want to be by the end of this year and start working towards it. For example, I want to be a virtuous woman: to be a virtuous woman you need to practice everything you are learning in this challenge and consistently do them. It should transcend into a lifestyle.

Declare After Me: I Can Be More! This Year I Will Be More!!! I Will Do More!!!

DAY 6

#CHALLENGE 2: *"When she speaks, she has something worthwhile to say, and she always says it kindly" (Proverbs 31:26, MSG).*

Good day Virtuous Woman. From our scripture in focus, a virtuous woman is kind. One of the synonyms of the word "kind" is "care". Care simply means to show concern, consideration, attention, thought, regard and sympathy. As a virtuous woman, anyone that comes in contact with you should attest to the fact that you are caring and that you show concern. To care means to put aside what you are going through and instead think of what others around you are going through and find ways to help them. To achieve this, you must love others as you love yourself. Many of us haven't learnt how to love ourselves and the truth is that you can't give what you don't have. If you don't genuinely have love, you can't show love to another person. So, the first question you need to ask yourself is this, Do I love myself? If you do, then treat others the way you treat yourself. If you don't love yourself, ask God to teach you how to love you. It is only after you have learnt to love yourself that you will be able to love another person.

ACTIVITY 1: Look for ways of caring and paying attention to the needs, challenges and problems of those living with you or in your neighbourhood. For example, in what ways can you help your domestic staff or nanny become a better person today?

Write them down below:

_____

_____

_____

_____

_____

Instead of always complaining and raising your voice over what they didn't get right, how can you help them get it right and improve?

.

ACTIVITY 2: Pray for the people that live with you or the people that live in your neighbourhood.

Prayer Focus: O Lord, teach me how to care for others. Help me to see less of my own challenges and issues and see more of what the people around me are going through, then use me to help them in Jesus name. Amen!!!

Chapter

04

CAREER

FINANCE

LIFESTYLE

MINISTRY

FAMILY

Chapter Four

EARLY BIRD

#CHALLENGE 3: *"She riseth also while it is yet night, and giveth meat to her household, and a portion to her maidens"*
(Proverbs 31:15 KJV).

There is a belief that the 21st century woman is busier and wiser than our mothers of old. We think that our mothers had more time on their hands and maybe because they weren't as educated as we are, they didn't know better and allowed the men to control them. However, our interest isn't about what our mothers did as much as what the bible tells us that this Woman did. Our standard isn't what the world does or says; our standard should be formed and drawn from the bible. We take our cue from God's word and we run with it despite what people say, think or postulate.

This woman wakes up before it is morning. It is only this kind of woman that will rise at night, meaning that the people living with her were awake as well. There is a generation that rise at night and their household feeds. The reason why your household is hungry is because you have not learnt how to rise at night. You need to understand that prayers made in the day and at night are not the same. There is something about waking up in the night to pray. Anyone who prays at night, can't come out in the day and be a victim of the decisions that men made at night.

Purpose is calling and you don't have time to waste. It's also important that you don't leave the total running of your home to the domestic staff or your husband to do it on your behalf. It is our responsibility as women to take care of our homes and be aware and in charge of what goes on in our homes whether we are physically present or not.

The first things to do when you wake up before dawn are:
- Have your quiet time: spend quality time with God in prayers and in the Word that is if you don't already wake up at midnight to pray.
- Make breakfast for your family even when you aren't eating. Make sure your children and husband have what to eat.
- Get your children ready for school. You can be of help to your husband by finding out what he would need you to help him with before you both leave for work or just before you return.
- Organize your day: Prepare a To-do list; plan the activities for the day for yourself and for those working in your home. Assign duties to them.

I met a couple recently who were having problems in their home and apparently the bone of contention was that the support his wife gave him when they got married stopped when they had their first baby. Her baby was over eight months at the time and let me add, she had a "help" at home. She stopped making breakfast for him and he had to go to work each day without breakfast or a lunch pack. While he got ready for work, she usually would still be well tucked in bed because she wasn't working and would always give the excuse that she was awake taking care of the baby during the night. Now let's paint a different scenario of what the Proverbs 31 Woman will do in our contemporary times. She would get up early and make breakfast for her husband and ensure his needs are met. Once he leaves the house for the office, she can either go back to sleep if she really didn't get enough rest during the night and if her baby is still asleep, or she starts the day's activities and goes to rest when next her baby falls asleep during the day.

The time spent with God is the time your strength is renewed. It is the time God increases your strength.

We must deliberately make waking up early in the morning a habit especially for those of us that have little children. Your "Me" time with God is very important if you are going to successfully create balance in your life. The time spent with God is the time your strength is renewed. It is the time God increases your strength. Trust me, you can't successfully become this Woman, if God doesn't strengthen you physically, spiritually, mentally and in every other way. You need God now more than ever before.

You need time as well to do your morning devotions with your family, prepare your children for school and prepare breakfast for your household. You also need your alone time each morning to get your thoughts together and get yourself organized so that you can have a productive day. So, you see why you can't afford to allow sleep rule and control you. Proverbs 6:10-11 says, "Yet a little sleep, a little slumber, a little folding of the hands to sleep:So, shall thy poverty come as one that travelleth, and thy want as an armed man.

Tips on waking up early:

- Ask and rely on the Holy Ghost to help you wake up early.
- Always remember to set your alarm or get someone to wake you up if you find it difficult to hear when your alarm rings.
- Always have a light meal in the night. You will find it easier to wake up in the night.
- When you have purpose on your mind, your purpose will keep you awake, and drive sleep out of your eyes. Discover purpose!
- Understanding that you are a role model to your children. Your children will emulate you. Be cautious of the lifestyle you are modeling for your children. Your children will remember what they saw you do more than what you told them.

Another scripture that is such a blessing is Proverbs 20:13 (BSB) and it says, "Do not love sleep, or you will grow poor; open your eyes and you will have plenty of food". Anyone who loves sleep will end up poor and will become hungry. Many of us have slept more hours than we have been productive. Always remember, while you are sleeping, there is someone awake making productive use of his or her time, and such a person will always be ahead of you. The bible says in Galatians 6:7 (KJV), "whatsoever a man soweth, that shall he also reap"; emphasis is on why it is important to sow rightly. If you sow sleep, you will reap poverty; but if you sow staying awake and being productive, you will reap abundance.

Our time must begin to make money and wealth for us. We need to be like this woman that understood the value and reward of staying awake. We were also told that she worked far into the night" (Proverbs 31: 18, MSG).

Career and ministry women are usually pressed for time especially when they are married as well. As a woman in career, business or ministry, or in all three, you will have to go to work, and also attend to your family matters. Most times 24 hours doesn't seem to be enough. Therefore, you need to plan, organize and execute. Don't procrastinate. I have discovered that organized people are more productive, efficient and effective than unorganized people. The time it will take an unorganized person to act is usually costly due to lack of planning, while the organized person will always achieve better results.

PRAYER FOCUS

The Proverbs 31 Woman and Her Health.

- O Lord, *today I ask for increase in strength and renewed strength. I declare, I receive power in all I do in Jesus name.*
- O Lord, *I decree, I will always be in good health. I decree, my health will never deteriorate in the name of Jesus. Everything that fights my health, today I command you to cease in the name of Jesus.*
- *Any disease associated with women that has manifested or is yet to manifest in my life, today I command them to die. Breast cancer, die; cervical cancer, die; any kind of cancer, die; infertility, die; any disease or sickness that wants to show up 5 years from now, 10 years from now, 20 years from now, I command them to die in the name of Jesus.*
- O Lord, *I decree I will not die prematurely in the name of Jesus. I will live to fulfill purpose in the name of Jesus.*

PRAYER FOCUS

- *I decree, I am a Proverbs 31 Woman. Anything standing in the way of my journey to becoming this Woman, today I command you to disappear in the name of Jesus.*
- *I receive the wisdom, knowledge, intelligence, strength, temperament to live up to God's expectations for my life in the name of Jesus.*
- *Today, I decree over every female member of my family, you will be a Virtuous Woman in the name of Jesus. I disconnect you from every wrong relationship or association in the name of Jesus.*
- *Every female family member, I decree you will fulfill purpose and destiny. No one will be a mediocre. No one will end up average. They will be career women and owners of conglomerates. They will be Ministry Women. No female member of my family will die small in the name of Jesus.*
- *Today, I decree, none of the female members of my family will marry foolish men, wicked men, selfish men, women beaters, women cheaters. Today, I decree, they will marry good men, God fearing men, faithful men and successful men in the name of Jesus.*

Amen!!!

ACTIVITIES

DAY 1

#CHALLENGE 3: *"She's up before dawn, preparing breakfast for her family and organizing her day" (Proverbs 31:15, MSG).*

ACTIVITY 1: Prepare a menu/food roster for your home. Make sure it is easily accessible for everyone, especially your domestic staff. Even if you do not have a domestic staff, still prepare a roster for yourself; it will guide you on what to cook.

- Plan on when you want to go shopping: monthly, bi-monthly, quarterly, or twice a year. Choose what is convenient for you.
- Even though you have a food roster, please tweak it or change it from time to time. The Proverbs 31 Woman in our time would deliberately modify her family's meal occasionally. Add some adventure to your meal plan. Let it not be monotonous and boring.

ACTIVITY 2: Prepare a roster for house chores. Your roster should cover Monday to Sunday.

ACTIVITY 3: Start your day by preparing a To-do list for yourself. Be disciplined and committed to it. Remember, the Proverbs 31 Woman's day starts at 12 Midnight.

_____

_____

_____

_____

Chapter

05

CAREER

FINANCE

LIFESTYLE

MINISTRY

FAMILY

Chapter Five

GENTLENESS

#CHALLENGE 4: *"She girdeth her loins with strength, and strengtheneth her arms."*
(Proverbs 31:17 KJV).

The strength referred to in this scripture isn't physical strength or outward physique, but it is an inner strength that builds character, carriage, and capacity. We are called the weaker vessel when it has to do with our physical looks; but when the going gets tough, we put on a strength that comes from within. It isn't about how you look, you don't need to have muscles and carry a 50kg dumbbell on both hands to prove that you are strong. Rather, there is a strength that can withstand the storms of life that could be domiciled inside the most fragile looking person.

In today's contemporary times, the Proverbs 31 Woman is that woman who has strength of character. She would rather go and work with her hands than sleep around for a meal or for material possessions. She would rather give her time and energy to work and patiently grow through the ranks than to offer her body sexually for promotion. This woman's strength isn't man-made but God-made. It is a strength gotten

THE PROVERBS 31 WOMAN IN CONTEMPORARY TIMES

from the place of an intimate walk with God. It isn't a strength that brags, nags, fights or shouts to be heard but it is a strength that understands how to use her inner virtues to get undeniable and amazing results. I remember in my early years in marriage, I used to exercise a lot of physical strength by shouting and being disrespectful to the extent that my husband would refer to me in Igbo parlance, "strong woman". Just in case you think it was a compliment, it wasn't; rather, it reaffirmed his disappointment in my attitude. In fact, I have come to learn and appreciate after many years that the beauty of a woman lies within.

> **The same effort we put to look good or attractive or externally should be the same effort (if not more), so that we look beautiful and attractive internally.**

The bible says in 1 Peter 3:3-4, (NASB) "Your adornment must not be merely external – braiding the hair, and wearing gold jewelry, or putting on dresses; but let it be the hidden person of the heart, with the imperishable quality of a gentle and quiet spirit, which is precious in the sight of God". To adorn is to beautify; it means to be made attractive by using decoration or enhancements. So as women, when we wear ornaments of precious jewels, dress up, style our hair and wear our cosmetics, the sole aim is to beautify ourselves. It is meant to make us look more attractive. These are all good, but the bible says that our beautification should not end with the external. The same effort we put to look good or attractive externally should be the same effort (if not more), so that we look beautiful and attractive internally. For us to adorn internally, we must learn how to beautify our hearts with the right virtues like a gentle and quiet spirit. Her strength isn't external but internal.

A Gentle and Quiet Spirit

Gentleness means to be constant and clear minded across all manner of situations. There is nothing strong about a person who is quick to lose temper and resort to aggression and violence in their spirit, words and actions. It is in fact a display of profound weakness. The opposite of gentleness is mindless aggression and violence. Gentleness is power under control. The truth is that there are some people who have cultivated a gentle and quiet spirit over the years while there are some who are yet to begin this journey. These definitions and lists of qualities aren't here to scare you or make you want to give up before trying or make you think it's a herculean task; rather, it's to trigger the "I can do all things" mentality within you. It just means you have a lot of work to do and there's no time to waste.

Another truth about gentleness is that a gentle word can calm the harshest response. The Bible in Proverbs 15:1 puts it this way, "A gentle answer turns away wrath, but a harsh word stirs up anger". To give a gentle answer is not saying what we want to say in the heat of an argument, no matter how much we want to say it, or how true it is. Gentleness is the ability to know when to speak and when to be silent, and being okay with both. When the bible tells us to possess a quiet spirit, it is referring to the state of your heart.

Kimberly Wagner adapted this definition from Matthew Henry's book titled "A Quest for Meekness and Quietness of Spirit" which states that "Gentleness is a calm confidence, settled assurance and rest of the soul. It is the tranquil stillness of a heart that is at rest in Christ. It is the place of peace. It springs from a heart of humility, radiating the fragrance of Christ".

Qualities of a gentle spirit:

- Peaceful
- Consistency of Character
- Not volatile or abrupt in your response to the world
- They aren't reactionary
- They don't respond immediately
- They are strong and full of self-control (they choose if and how to react)

How to develop strength found in gentleness:

1. **Be conscious of your feelings:** Pretending will not make your feelings disappear. It will only push those feelings beneath the surface. It is important that you are honest with yourself about your feelings.

    - Ask yourself - how am I feeling right here and now? You can find answers by how your body is responding. For instance, you may have feelings of being tensed or stressed.
    - What is your body telling you about how you feel in your mind?

2. **Use the space between stimulus and response:** Gentle people make and embrace the time and space between something happening and when they respond to it. They stop and take a metaphorical step back to ground themselves within that moment between the stimulus (something happens to them) and the response (they decide what they are going to do about it).

3. **Take your focus deeper:** A gentle person will always find reasons that will ignite a positive motivation. They find reasons

to say, yes, this is worth my attention and investment. They are aware of a deeper sense of purpose so that when it feels futile or meaningless, they can draw on a reason to continue that transcends their own ability to muster energy.

4. **Decide what you are going to do:** Rather than reacting, gentle spirits embrace their ability to choose. Gentleness has insight to see implications and consequences of actions. The action is taken now with a good idea of what will happen as a result of what is done. The rational decision is usually taken at the expense of a regrettable emotive reaction.

5. **Follow Up with anyone else affected:** Having empathy and an understanding that the world doesn't revolve around their perception of reality, is a habit of the gentle spirit. Empathy comes through gentle strength; by seeking to experience the world through their lenses, you find a place to make a profound difference in their lives. I stumbled on this quote (author unknown) that sums it up, "Be kind/gentle, for everyone you meet is fighting a difficult battle".

6. **Allow yourself to care:** A person with a gentle spirit acknowledges and allows him or herself to care about things - other people, the world, their hopes and dreams. When you have experienced hurt, or you have been let down, or taken for granted, it becomes easier to turn off or become disenfranchised and begin to resent the emotional and physical effort that you are spending. We must deliberately make the decision to care.

How to possess a gentle and quiet spirit

- By constantly feeding your mind with the word of God.
- By practicing gentleness and quietness of spirit in your everyday life.
- We practice these traits as we interact with the people in our lives. Each day holds situations where we need to offer a gentle word. Each day also contains mishaps that reveal if our spirits are still at peace.
- By having a robust prayer life.
- By shifting your focus to God and intentionally decide not to spend time and energy on matters that are not destiny related.

The Proverbs 31 Woman is a self-motivator. She strengthens her arms. She encourages herself to do more work and be more in life. She isn't waiting for the accolades or recognition of men to do her work. She isn't relying on other people's accomplishments but she pushes herself to be more. She doesn't need to be pressured to go to work or to take care of her husband and children. She is enthusiastic, interested and strives to become more.

> **She encourages herself to do more work and be more in life.**

To be self-motivated means you will need to be disciplined and focused. You must be passionate about what you do. Self-motivated people do not get distracted. In contemporary times, as women we must avoid distractions from friends and our environment. Anybody that can't motivate you to be better or inspire you positively shouldn't be in your circle. The Proverbs 31 Woman is hard working and energetic. She doesn't avoid responsibilities and is always accountable.

PRAYER FOCUS

- O Lord, *I receive today the spirit of humility. Every seed of arrogance and pride operating in my life, today I command you to disappear in Jesus name.*
- O Lord, *help me become this Proverbs 31 Woman. I receive today the inner strength of a gentle and quiet spirit in the name of Jesus.*
- O Lord, *surround me with friends or the right people that will help grow the right virtues in me in the name of Jesus.*
- O Lord, *I disconnect from every relationship that discourages me from possessing this inner strength in the name of Jesus.*
- O Lord, *I will not die small. Every power that wants me to stay small and not amount to anything, today I cut you down in the name of Jesus.*
- O Lord, *please give me the grace and strength to always wake up very early and go to bed very late without breaking down in health or mind in the name of Jesus.*
- O Lord, *any weakness in me, today I decree, let it be converted to strength in the name of Jesus.*
- O Lord, *increase my sensitivity in the spirit in the name of Jesus. I will know what is happening around me per time. I will not walk in the dark in the name of Jesus. Expose whatever needs to be exposed in my home, business, career and family in the name of Jesus.*

Amen! Amen! Amen!

ACTIVITIES

DAY 1

#CHALLENGE 4: *"She girdeth her loins with strength, and strengtheneth her arms" (Proverbs 31:17, KJV).*

ACTIVITY 1: What are you doing with your time?

_____

_____

_____

- The Proverbs 31 Woman in today's society wouldn't have time to sit and watch television all day or most part of the day. She wouldn't have time to gossip and browse unproductively on social media. She wouldn't always have the time to sleep as much as she would want to.
- Successful people do not have time to waste time. The reason some people aren't successful yet is because they still have idle time and need to effectively maximize it.

ACTIVITY 2: Build good character. Learn and know when to refrain from talking and when to speak. Your refusal to respond to an issue does not mean you are a fool or that you will be taken for granted. There are situations that don't deserve your response. Ignore such situations with a quiet and gentle disposition.

Chapter

06

CAREER

FINANCE

LIFESTYLE

MINISTRY

FAMILY

GROW

#CHALLENGE 5: *"She perceiveth that her merchandise is good: her candle goeth not out by night."*
(Proverbs 31:18 KJV).

The bible says in Proverbs 20:27 (KJV), "The spirit of man is the candle of the Lord". In other words, this candle is bigger than just her candle. At night, there are things she begins to weigh about her career, business, ministry, etcetera. She isn't worrying about them or anxious about the different areas of her life. She uses the night time to settle her accounts, strategize, plan and prepare for execution. Still at night, there are things she removes and there are things she plants: she does this because she has an understanding that while men slept, the enemy sowed tares. She is mindful of her competitors. She is mindful of attacks that could come. She is mindful of pitfalls and mistakes that could come as a result of not taking due diligence so she spends time at night to ensure no stone is left unturned.

She also uses the night seasons to improve on herself. She uses that time to build capacity, grow and become more. Do not let all you can become be what people can see now. You are more than who you are now. You are more than this current level you are operating at. Never imagine that you are little. The bible says in Romans 12:2 (KJV), "And be not conformed to this world: but be ye transformed by the renewing of your mind, that ye may prove what is that good, and acceptable, and perfect will of God". You definitely need an increase in capacity to become a Proverbs 31 woman and there is no place that increases your capacity to be more like the place of prayer. Some of us don't understand the concept of prayer, so it is still a religious activity. There are realms you get into while speaking in the Holy Ghost, and uncommon ideas begin to enter your spirit and mind.

The bible says in 1 Corinthians 14:2 (KJV), "For he that speaketh in an unknown tongue speaketh not unto men, but unto God: for no man understandeth him; howbeit in the spirit he speaketh mysteries". The word "mysteries" means to download purposes and programmes. The purposes of God are downloaded into your mind while you pray in the Holy Ghost. When you think it's time to think about your business or career start speaking in the Holy Ghost. An idea that has never existed will drop into your mind. The bible says there's nothing new under the sun, but I must say that there's everything new above the sun.

The purposes of God are downloaded into your mind while you pray in the Holy Ghost.

This woman knows that her merchandise is good, and that is why she stays awake at night. As a Proverbs 31 Woman, you need to understand why your candle can't go out at night. For everything you do, there is someone somewhere that wants to copy it or that will copy it. Everything you do that is good, someone will copy it and may God help you if they do theirs louder that you. When they copy, they blow it and people may even think you were the one that copied it from them. So it's important you stay awake to receive fresh ideas, wisdom and insight so that you are ten steps ahead of those who want to copy you.

I love the Proverbs 31 Woman because she knows how to maximize her night season. She doesn't stay up late to watch movies or get entertained on social media or to catch up with the latest juicy gossip, but she puts her time to productive use. Our scripture focus also says that she is energetic and a hard worker, which explains partly why she stays awake in the night. It will take only hard-working people to be busy working while most people are resting or misappropriating the use of time.

It will take only women on an assignment to stay awake after their husbands and children have gone to bed. It will take only women who are running with purpose to go the extra mile after having a tiring and exhausting day, and still keep the candle burning instead of calling it quits for the day. The Proverbs 31 Woman in today's society isn't just an ordinary woman. She is a woman that is passionate, purposeful and is on an assignment. Your passion, your assignment, and your purpose are what will keep you tireless, enthusiastic, active and alert when your body should naturally be worn out after a long busy day. In this journey of becoming the Proverbs 31 Woman,

> **The Proverbs 31 Woman in today's society isn't just an ordinary woman. She is a woman that is passionate, purposeful and is on assignment.**

you must come to terms with who you are, where you are going, what God wants you to be doing now, and who God has called you to be.

The interesting thing about the Proverbs 31 Woman is that she is highly competent and a successful woman. She is the woman who has mastered too many things and does them with ease.

ACTIVITIES

DAY 1

#CHALLENGE 5: *"She perceiveth that her merchandise is good: her candle goeth not out by night." (Proverbs 31:18 KJV)*.

ACTIVITY 1: What is your purpose?

_____

_____

_____

ACTIVITY 2: What is your assignment?

_____

_____

_____

ACTIVITY 3: What are you passionate about?

_____

_____

_____

ACTIVITY 4: Don't go to bed early. Stay awake into the night praying, planning, reading, discovering you, and developing yourself.

_____

_____

_____

DAY 2

#CHALLENGE 5: *"She perceiveth that her merchandise is good: her candle goeth not out by night." (Proverbs 31:18 KJV).*

ACTIVITY 1: Find out new vendors selling the products you need at affordable and cheaper rates than you have been currently procuring. However, be careful that they still maintain the quality of the products you desire.

- Find out new ways of buying to save cost. For example, you can engage in bulk purchasing where you contribute money in groups, buy and share amongst yourselves. However, this will have to be done with trusted friends or colleagues.
- For some of us, if it isn't an urgent need, you can wait for the sales season to buy that piece of furniture, clothes, etcetera.

ACTIVITY 2: Write out the skills you possess?

_____

_____

_____

ACTIVITY 3: On a scale of 1 to 10, how good are you at each of the skills you have listed? (1 being the lowest, and 10 being the highest)

_____

_____

_____

_____

ACTIVITY 4: Are your skills generating income for you?

_____

_____

_____

ACTIVITY 5: If you answered Yes, is it possible to increase the income you are getting from the skill(s)? How?

If you answered *No*, how can you get your skill(s) to generate income for you?

_____

_____

_____

_____

Chapter

07

CAREER

FINANCE

LIFESTYLE

MINISTRY

FAMILY

INTEGRITY

#CHALLENGE 6: *"She shops around for the best yarns and cottons, and enjoys knitting and sewing."* *(Proverbs 31:13 MSG).*

Interestingly, the Proverbs 31 Woman is a very skillful woman. She knew where to get the best yarns, and cottons. In other words, she buys very good quality materials for her manufacturing outfit to make the products (dresses) she is going to sell in her factory. She doesn't buy poor quality or bad quality materials in order to make quick gains. This action of hers implies that she is a woman of integrity or what we could call high moral standards. She is thorough and more interested in building a sustainable business. In her dealings with the outside world, she is futuristic in the way she thinks.

As you walk towards becoming a virtuous woman, you must begin to work from the future to the present. Whatever you are doing presently, whether in your marriage, career, business, relationships, etcetera, the picture of the future of that given endeavor should determine the decisions you take now. We need to be careful so that we do not jeopardize our future by our present-day actions.

Your work isn't about eating just for today but should be about laying a legacy, and having an institution. You need to build empires that will stand the test of time. You need something that is sustainable and durable and this is achieved when you build structures, systems and possess integrity. Your business must have a competitive edge or advantage. You need to discover what is unique to you and to your business. Why will someone leave your competitors to buy your own product? This woman knows how to carve a niche for herself in the market place.

She has various ways of generating resources that will ensure that she is never stranded.

I love the Good News Translation that says she keeps herself busy making wool and linen cloth. In the time that she could be idling away, she engages herself skillfully. I have said this earlier, and permit me to repeat it again: this woman we are becoming has no time for idle talk, gossip, laziness, spending all her time on watching movies, social media, etcetera. There are activities that are 'time wasters', and this woman will have none of them encroach into her day. Once she is done with her 9 to 5 job, or her regular chores, she finds other kinds of work *(knitting and sewing)* to keep her busy. The Proverbs 31 Woman has multiple streams of income. She has various ways of generating resources that will ensure that she is never stranded.

PRAYER FOCUS

The Proverbs 31 Woman and Her Finances.

- O Lord, *today, I receive fresh and uncommon ideas that will usher me into higher dimensions of financial breakthrough.*
- O Lord, *whatever business and career I go ahead to do will yield multiple favours and unprecedented financial increase for me.*
- O Lord, *let the oil of high favour distinguish everything and everyone connected to me in the name of Jesus.*
- *I have more. I gain new grounds. I am financially independent in the name of Jesus.*
- O Lord, *bless me to be a blessing to others and to kingdom assignments in the name of Jesus.*
- *Today, I receive the power to make wealth. I receive the grace to connect to business partners, financial giants, and intellectual giants in the name of Jesus.*
- *Every platform I need in this season of my life, today I decree let them open up to me in the name of Jesus.*
- *I will not beg. I will not lack. I will not borrow. I receive the grace to lend to nations in the name of Jesus.*
- *Everything that makes me live above my means today, I receive the discipline of the Lord. I will not spend what I do not have.*
- O Lord, *I receive the grace to be a prudent wife/woman. I refuse to be wasteful in the name of Jesus.*
- O Lord, *any trace of greed, gluttony, selfishness in me; today I repent of them in the name of Jesus.*

Amen! Amen! Amen!

ACTIVITIES

DAY 1

#CHALLENGE 6: *"She shops around for the best yarns and cottons, and enjoys knitting and sewing." (Proverbs 31:13 MSG).*

ACTIVITY 1: Who is running your home?

_____

_____

_____

- Is it your husband, a domestic staff, relatives, siblings, mother, or friend? If you aren't the one, please take back ownership of your home; take back the responsibility of running your home.
- It's time to take full responsibility for your home while those helping you can assist you when you need their services.

ACTIVITY 2: Decide today those chores you will do by yourself and the ones you will leave for others. Basically, know what you must do each day except when you are not in town.

_____

_____

_____

_____

_____

_____

ACTIVITY 3: Discover what you enjoy doing and incorporate it into your schedule.

_____

_____

_____

ACTIVITY 4: What can you enjoy doing, fetch you some money? Can you build a business empire from it?

_____

_____

_____

ACTIVITY 5: Today, make sure you identify and avoid time wasters e.g. friends who you spend unproductive time with, watching movies, idle talk, or gossiping.

_____

_____

_____

- Consciously ensure that you can account for almost every second, minute, hour of today.
- Use your time wisely and profitably.
- Find ways to make sure that 'time' works for you today and not the other way round e.g. Let time make money for you, grow you, improve you, and bring value into your life.

Declare After Me: Time will work for me today. I will keep myself productively occupied in Jesus' Name.

Chapter

08

CAREER   FINANCE   LIFESTYLE   MINISTRY   FAMILY

DISCERNMENT

#CHALLENGE 7: "She looks over a field and buys it,
then with the money she's put aside, plants a garden."
(Proverbs 31:16 MSG).

This verse in the King James Version says that "she considereth a field". The word consider from the original Hebrew is she "discerns". When she discerns it, then it will be fruitful. Many people have made major career and business mistakes because they were not discerning. Whenever you give this woman an offer to take a loan, start a new line of business, invest in a business, she doesn't just jump at the offer or ideas but takes her time to discern it. She doesn't make financial mistakes. She discerns her season. She knows at what point to invest and when not to.

You need to be discerning. A woman who is running a prophetic business knows the time to release a fresh energy of the spirit. You definitely need discernment especially in times like this. The Proverbs 31 Woman shows us how being a woman should be – spiritual, insightful, super amazing and extremely attractive. She is definitely a woman of many awesome parts. She epitomizes hard work, diligence, intelligence, wisdom, prudence, strength, humility, discipline, goodness and kindness. She is financially prudent and not an impulsive buyer or spender. For every dime she spends, it is always a well calculated decision. This becomes difficult to practice for some of us because the banking and credit firms are encouraging us to live on credit, and to live above our income. They offer loans at high interest rates which leaves the debtor broke at the end of each month. She wasn't a debtor; she lived within her means. This woman was a content woman; she grew her finances to such a point where she could afford to buy what she needed.

> **The level of wastage has increased today, that many of us buy what we do not need and end up throwing them away while they are many people in need of that same item...**

It doesn't stop there, when you walk through the shopping malls and the internet, there seems to always be one discount or sales taking place that looks pretty attractive. Most times, we are made to believe that it's better to buy that piece of item at that time because it is being sold at a discounted price without considering whether it is a need or want. Most times, we don't buy what we need; we just buy because it's supposedly cheaper. So, people are compelled to buy groceries that stay in their refrigerators or home and expire without them using it. The level of wastage has increased today, that many of us buy what we do not need and end up throwing them away while there are many people in need of that same item or product but can't afford to buy it.

Please don't get me wrong, all of these are good if we are disciplined and know how to put them to good use. However, many of us are caught in this web of never having enough money to do the things we need to do. And for as long as we aren't sufficiently prudent in how we spend the resources we have; we will never be able to become this Proverbs 31 Woman. The Bible says in Proverbs 31:16 MSG that it is with the money she puts aside that she plants a garden. This means that she buys the field with her money then goes ahead and plants with her savings.

This brings me to the next question. Do you have a savings culture? How much have you saved so far? This is a rhetorical question which you need to answer for yourself. As one year ends and another year begins, how much can you boast (permit my use of word) that you have saved? If you have spent your savings, this question is for you. What did you spend your savings on? In our journey to becoming a Proverbs 31 Woman, you will need to develop a robust and healthy savings culture. You can achieve this by saving daily, weekly, monthly depending on what is convenient for you and the amount you will put aside will depend on your current financial level. However, if you are looking to save conveniently, the truth is that you will never save. For some of us, it will take a lot of discipline to achieve a savings culture but you can do it. Yes, you can!!!

The Proverbs 31 Woman thinks trans-generational
Many young women believe that it is only the man that should spend on capital projects and not the woman. The first part of the verse tells us that she is an investor and goes about looking for opportunities for good investments. She takes decisions on purchasing assets with her own money. Her money isn't just for clothes, jewelries, hairs and other

material possessions. She thinks trans-generational. It's no longer just about her but also about the future of the next generation. She is focused on the future. She doesn't wait for the future to meet her unprepared. She doesn't just live in the now and she recognizes that not every money she gets is a harvest. She understands the difference between her seed and her harvest. She is aware that at times her money is a seed and ensures that she doesn't eat her seed.

In our society today, there is this erroneous mindset that a woman's money is for her alone and the man's money is for everyone including his wife. We have wives who contribute little or nothing to the running of their homes; but the Proverbs 31 Woman knows that she isn't in a competition with her husband on who is responsible for what, but whatever she can afford to do for the family, she goes ahead and does it without making a fuss about it.

Really, if we want to be honest with ourselves, it sounds like this Woman in the bible was the one doing most of the work, while the bible only tells us of how her husband sat at the gates. However, we know that the gates in the oriental culture was where the elders met to deliberate and judge cases and settle the issues and problems of the people. Apparently, for her husband to be one of the men at the gate suggests that he was highly respected and must have been very successful to be considered as one of the men at the gate. A perfect example of this is Boaz (in the book of Ruth); the bible tells us that Boaz was a man that sat at the gates; however, he was a very wealthy business

"Meanwhile Boaz went up to the town gate and sat down there just as the guardian-redeemer a' *he had mentioned came along. Boaz said, "Come over here, my friend, and sit down." So he went over and sat down.*

²Boaz took ten of the elders of the town and said, "Sit here," and they did so.³ Then he said to the guardian-redeemer, "Naomi, who has come back from Moab, is selling the piece of land that belonged to our relative Elimelek.⁴ I thought I should bring the matter to your attention and suggest that you buy it in the presence of these seated here and in the presence of the elders of my people. If you will redeem it, do so. But if you|ᵇ| will not, tell me, so I will know. For no one has the right to do it except you, and I am next in line."

"I will redeem it," he said.

⁵Then Boaz said, "On the day you buy the land from Naomi, you also acquire Ruth the Moabite, the|ᶜ| dead man's widow, in order to maintain the name of the dead with his property."

⁶At this, the guardian-redeemer said, "Then I cannot redeem it because I might endanger my own estate. You redeem it yourself. I cannot do it."

⁷(Now in earlier times in Israel, for the redemption and transfer of property to become final, one party took off his sandal and gave it to the other. This was the method of legalizing transactions in Israel.)

⁸So the guardian-redeemer said to Boaz, "Buy it yourself." And he removed his sandal.

⁹Then Boaz announced to the elders and all the people, "Today you are witnesses that I have bought from Naomi all the property of Elimelek, Kilion and Mahlon.¹⁰I have also acquired Ruth the Moabite, Mahlon's widow, as my wife, in order to maintain the name of the dead with his property, so that his name will not disappear from among his family or from his hometown. Today you are witnesses!"

¹¹Then the elders and all the people at the gate said, "We are witnesses. May the LORD make the woman who is coming into your home like Rachel and Leah, who together built up the family of Israel. May you have standing in

Ephrathah and be famous in Bethlehem.[12] *Through the offspring the LORD gives you by this young woman, may your family be like that of Perez, whom Tamar bore to Judah." (Ruth 4:1-12, NIV)*

This Woman married a responsible man. She married a man that had integrity and high moral standards. She attracted her kind. As young ladies, please marry a responsible man. A man that fears God and has high moral standards is definitely better than just going for the money. There are men like the bible will speak about in Luke 18:2: "Saying, there was in a certain city a judge who did not fear God or regard man". As a judge, he must have been financially stable but to be married to one who didn't fear God or have regard for man is a worst condition to be in. Your money won't save you. Another unfortunate pair in the bible is Abigail and Nabal. She was married to a wealthy man who was foolish. Young ladies, be careful what drives your affections towards who you would want to spend the rest of your life with. It is important to pray for a well- rounded man as you trust God to get married soon. It is very important that the man has a job. Even the bible says in 1 Timothy 5:8, "But if any provide not for his own, and especially for those of his own house, he hath denied the faith, and is worse than an infidel". So even in the New Testament, men are not expected to be idle. An idle man is compared to a man who is an unbeliever.

It is important to pray for a well-rounded man as you trust God to get married soon.

Another interesting part of this verse which is also a powerful tip on saving is "with money she's put aside", meaning that when you put aside, you ignore and act like that thing doesn't exist. It's like keeping money where you cannot access it when you feel like but money kept aside has an assignment or has its maturity date so you will have to wait for it.

It's time for us to become disciplined with our finances. No more impulsive shopping when passing the shopping malls. I know that may be a bit difficult, but I assure you, you can do it. The bible says in Philippians 4:13 NKJV "I can do all things through Christ who strengthens me". Moving forward, buy *only* what you need and *only* what you budgeted for.

When reading Proverbs 31:16 NIV, the bible says, "out of her earnings she plants a vineyard". Earning from the Cambridge English Dictionary is defined as the amount of money that someone is paid for working. It is the same thing as income, salary or wages. It is important that every woman gets a job or starts a business that she would be paid for daily, weekly or monthly. The idea here is not about when you are paid, or how you are paid, but just have a source of income. We shouldn't solely depend on a man or people to meet every of our need. We are meant to be contributors and not just collectors. I know some women are married to men who do not want them to work, and if you would love to work, pray about it. However, if your husband doesn't agree, please don't insist, or get bitter, nag or complain but patiently wait for him to agree whenever God permits. As you keep praying about it, someday it will happen. There are also men that pay their wives to stay at home which is fine, and for such women you don't necessarily need to look for a job because you are earning a living.

PRAYER FOCUS

- O Lord, *today I receive the spirit of discernment. I have a discerning heart. I know what to do, I know how to do it, and I know when to do it in the name of Jesus.*
- O Lord, *I will be sensitive in the spirit. I decree, my spiritual gateways are opened now in the name of Jesus.*
- *Whatever is fighting my spiritual sensitivity from being sharp at all times, I command you to disappear now in the name of Jesus.*
- *My spirit man, I decree, you will no longer be riotous and noisy in the name of Jesus. I align to hearing deep matters of the Spirit in the name of Jesus.*

Amen!!!

ACTIVITIES

DAY 1

#CHALLENGE 7: *"She looks over a field and buys it, then with the money she's put aside, plants a garden." (Proverbs 31:16 MSG).*

ACTIVITY 1: For those unemployed or who want to start a new business:
- Pray and ask God to give you a job.
- Ask God for the capital and other resources you need to start your business in the name of Jesus.

ACTIVITY 2: For those in employment:
- Ask God for a better paying job or a more challenging job (if needed) in the name of Jesus.
- Ask God for promotion this season.
- Pray for high favour and that those that matter will speak in your favour in the name of Jesus.

Finally, remember to save some money each month!!!

Chapter

09

CAREER   FINANCE   LIFESTYLE   MINISTRY   FAMILY

Chapter Nine

PROACTIVE

#CHALLENGE 8: *"She doesn't worry about her family when it snows; their winter clothes are all mended and ready to wear" (Proverbs 31:21 MSG).*

e are being introduced to another awesome quality of the Proverbs 31 Woman. She reminds me of the onion which reveals a fresh layer after every peel. Our scripture focus is on Proverbs 31:21 MSG, "She doesn't worry about her family when it snows; their winter clothes are all mended and ready to wear." From this scripture, we can see that this woman is always prepared and doesn't panic at the change in seasons because she prepares for it. The winter season is the coldest season amongst all the seasons and most times considered as the harshest of the four weathers. The Proverbs 31 Woman is prepared to face the challenges of life and always battle ready. She never shies away from responsibilities or problems. She willingly faces life's pressure with the determination to succeed and gets herself equipped to handle the different circumstances. The bible says in Ephesians 6:11 KJV "Put on the whole armour of God, that ye may be able to stand against the wiles of the devil". There is a preparation needed to withstand the wiles of the enemy.

The place of prayer cannot be overemphasized for us as Virtuous Women. Our preparation isn't just physical but spiritual as well. The Virtuous Woman in today's society should be a woman that is sensitive to her environment. She is the woman that knows how to shield her family from the attacks of the devil. The next verse which is Ephesians 6:12 KJV says "For we wrestle not against flesh and blood, but against principalities, against powers, against the rulers of the darkness of this world, against spiritual wickedness in high places". Our prayer altars must always stay aflame. There should be no ashes on our altar. While others sleep, we are the ones awake and raising intercession for ourselves and for our children. Dear woman, after all is said and done, our children are all we have got, so it is wise that we spend time praying for them.

She is the woman who knows how to shield her family from the attacks of the devil.

This scripture in Proverbs 31:21 can also mean that she takes care of things before they become an emergency. She isn't "a last minute" kind of person. She does her preparations way in advance and quietly waits for the appropriate time to showcase all she has been doing quietly. Her opportunities meet her ready and well prepared. She prepares for herself and also prepares to accommodate her family members; peradventure any of her family members fail to prepare, her personal preparation covers for them. Most of us meet our moments or hours of visitation unprepared. God forbid that when God decides to announce you, you won't be ready.

She is aware that a time will come when her family will need to be kept warm and she starts way ahead of time to prepare for the season. We should never meet any season of our life unprepared. What preparations do we have to do today to secure our tomorrow and that of our spouses and children? For this woman, whether in spring, summer or autumn, she was already prepared for the winter season. Her children and husband's clothes were mended, ironed and ready to wear. For some of us, we don't take out time to sort our children's clothes, fix the torn ones, wash and iron them.

We can also say that the Proverbs 31 Woman isn't entangled with the spirit of procrastination. She does what she needs to do on time, without needless postponements. Avoid every form of procrastination. Procrastination says, I will do tomorrow what I should have done today. Procrastination brings you to your future or opportunities unprepared. Be deliberate today and choose not to walk in procrastination. Go about your daily activities with this mentality: whatever needs to be done, do it now.

Procrastination brings you to your future or opportunities unprepared.

The Proverbs 31 Woman is always ready in season and out of season. The goal of this challenge will be to learn how to be prepared for your big day or for the opportunities God will be bringing your way. I pray for you: may you never meet an opportunity unprepared in Jesus' name.

This woman is aware that it will definitely snow some day; even though it is summer now, she knows that after summer, there's autumn and winter. We may not know the particular day our opportunities will come or our day of visitation, but we know that it will come someday and very soon. For the bible says in Proverbs 23:18 KJV, "for surely there is an end; and thine expectation shall not be cut off". So, like the Proverbs 31 Woman, we act based on this knowledge. Whatsoever has a beginning will definitely have an end, and the end is so near.

Some of the synonyms of the word 'worry' are anxiety, disquiet, tension, nervousness, stress, and strain. Worry has a negative effect on our disposition, attitude and general outlook on life. The bible says in John 14:1 NIV "Do not let your hearts be troubled. You believe in God; believe also in me". The Proverbs 31 Woman has learnt how not to meditate on the wrong things. It is important that we keep watch over our hearts. When the enemy wants to get you, one of the first places he attacks is your heart. He knows that once he gets your heart, he can control you. No wonder Philippians 4:6-7 NIV says "Do not be anxious about anything, but in every situation, by prayer and petition, with thanksgiving, present your requests to God. And the peace of God, which transcends all understanding, will guard your hearts and your minds in Christ Jesus". So, it is the peace of God that guards (protects) our heart and mind. The next time you read Proverbs 4:23 NIV "Above all else, guard your heart, for everything you do flows from it", remember that the one that enables us to guard our heart is God.

The Proverbs 31 Woman has learnt not to meditate on wrong things. It is important that we watch over our hearts.

All we need in order for us to take charge and control of our heart is the peace of God. For everyone that works in the peace of God, no challenge, storm, or battle of life will be able to weigh such a person down. 1 Peter 5:7 NLV further adds, "Give all your worries and cares to God, for he cares about you." It is a deliberate action which we need to take especially as women. Most of the time, we are referred to as the emotional ones and we are in constant battle with our hearts and minds concerning what to believe, who to believe, when to believe and how to believe. We are encumbered with every other person's problem, from our husbands, children, siblings, friends and parents. At times you may feel insecure about your job, fear for your children's future, or be concerned with your health. So when God says "give me your worries and cares", it shows that He knows we would get worried but when the time comes, we should let go of it by giving it to him.

When we worry, it doesn't change anything. My husband Pastor Jerry usually will say that the same energy you use in worrying is the same energy that you need for meditation. Worry is negative meditation; so, convert it to a positive kind of meditation and I know God will answer you quickly. Rather than worry, meditate on God's word concerning that challenge and pray more about it. Taking the action of praying and meditating will produce tremendous results but worry will produce nothing, rather it has the ability to leave you sick.

Still on Proverbs 31:21, I noticed that she is completely selfless. She is more concerned with the needs of others than with hers. Other synonyms of the word "selfless" are self-denying, self-sacrificing, kind, generous, magnanimous, compassionate, open-handed, etcetera. For us to become virtuous women, we must always put others first before ourselves. I know the society says otherwise and encourages selfishness in our days, but we are citizens of heaven, where the Lord Jesus Christ lives (Philippians 3:20, NLV) and we need to act like it.

There are days our spouse, children, friends, colleagues, and people generally, will act or say things that will make you want to stop being kind, but please don't ever let their actions or inactions affect you negatively.

PRAYER FOCUS

- *My Father, my Father, cause me to be selfless/self-sacrificing towards my family in the name of Jesus.*
- *My Father, my Father, I cast all my cares on you. From today, I will stop worrying and start trusting you more in Jesus' name.*
- *O Lord, cause me to stay prepared and always ready in Jesus name. I will not miss out on any opportunity you bring my way in Jesus name.*
- *O Lord, even when the people around me don't appreciate my efforts, help me to remain selfless in the name of Jesus. I will not change negatively because of the bad treatments I receive from others.*
- *O Lord, whatsoever I do, may I always remember that I am doing it unto the Lord and not for the vain glory of man in the name of Jesus.*
- *O Lord, please bless me more that I may become a channel of blessing to all those around me in Jesus name. Amen! Amen! Amen!*

A Word of Encouragement

I want to encourage you, God sees, God knows and God hears. Please never get discouraged to the point of giving up. Your miracle/breakthrough is just a breath away; wait for it, it won't be long anymore.

We just read that the Proverbs 31 Woman is selfless, self-denying and self-sacrificing; all these point to the fact that she places others before herself. I want to encourage married women or any woman who has been through a season or lifetime of giving of oneself and in return received the opposite. Please don't get weary. The Bible says in Galatians 6:9 "And let us not be weary in well doing: for in due season we shall reap, if we faint not". There is a reaping coming your way if you don't give up. God's Word and promises never fall to the ground; for every good seed you have sown, there shall be a harvest.

Your future is predetermined by the seeds you sow today. There is no tomorrow without today.

ACTIVITIES

DAY 1

#CHALLENGE 8: *"She doesn't worry about her family when it snows; their winter clothes are all mended and ready to wear." (Proverbs 31:21 MSG).*

ACTIVITY 1: Hand over all your burdens to God; everything that makes you get worried and troubled whether it is your husband, relationships, children, finances, business, career or health.

• List them out

_____

_____

ACTIVITY 2: Clean out your children's, husband and your wardrobes. Sort out the clothes that they won't be wearing again into two piles; the first pile will be old clothes that are too old or damaged that can't be given out (if any) and the second pile will be old clothes that can be given out.

- Decide who you will give out the old clothes to: younger siblings, relatives, neighbours, friends, orphanage homes, charity or the less privileged.
- For the clothes that they can still wear, ensure that they are neatly tucked away in wardrobes and cupboards. Make sure that all the buttons are intact, torn areas are stitched and the clothes are well folded and preferably ironed and maintain it that way. It's usually embarrassing when you have to start amending clothes when you are a few hours or almost late to a meeting or to school.

DAY 2

#CHALLENGE 8: *"She doesn't worry about her family when it snows; their winter clothes are all mended and ready to wear." (Proverbs 31:21 MSG).*

ACTIVITY 1: Set aside what your children will wear throughout the week between Saturday and Sunday.

- You need to know where all their uniforms, shoes, socks and underwear are kept. Please ensure nothing should be hidden or forgotten or lost in hidden corners of the room or house.

ACTIVITY 2: Teach your children how to be responsible and accountable. Teach them how to arrange their wardrobes and how to wash and iron their clothes. Prepare them for their future. Start on time.

- Don't leave this training to the boarding secondary schools to do it for you. Start NOW; Do it yourself. Let the contributions made by your children's school be an addition and not the foundation.

Chapter

10

CAREER

FINANCE

LIFESTYLE

MINISTRY

FAMILY

Chapter Ten

BLESSED

#CHALLENGE 9: "Strength and honour are her clothing;
and she shall rejoice in time to come"
(Proverbs 31:25 KJV).

Our scripture focus says "Strength and honour are her clothing; and she shall rejoice in time to come". This Woman wears strength and dignity. What are we wearing? What are we clothed with? Whereas this Woman is clothed with strength and honour, some of us are clothed with envy, anger, strive, bitterness, frustration, weakness, tiredness, and emptiness, and we frown at tomorrow due to worry and apprehension. I believe problems have always existed ever since Adam and Eve sinned in the Garden of Eden. They introduced sufferings, hardships, challenges, and troubles to mankind. So, this Woman for whom Proverbs 31 says "Who can find a Virtuous Woman" was operating in a time that she had to deal with challenges as we are going through today. Ecclesiastes 1:9 NIV says, "What has been will be again, what has been done will be done again; there is nothing new under the sun".

According to Merriam Webster Dictionary, "Strength is the quality or state of being strong. It is the capacity for exertion or endurance. It is the power to resist force; it is the power to resist attack." The strength of a woman is seen in the way she handles challenging situations. Her strength isn't a physical type of strength, but it is that strength that comes from a quiet and gentle spirit. It is that strength that is composed in the midst of a storm. It is that strength that doesn't win battles through quarreling or arguing but by virtue of a calm disposition. As women, we may look weak, but we aren't weak. Even in our lowest states, God has clothed us with strength. Every woman should possess this quality- endurance.

The synonyms of the word "endurance" are *patience, staying power, determination, doggedness, stamina, tolerance and tenacity.* In marriage, in the running of our homes - handling our domestic staff, children, subordinates at work, etcetera, we must be women that can endure whatever situation that confronts us. We must show patience, dogged determination, staying power and tolerate people. We shouldn't respond or be known to respond with a "shout". Most times, when a person shouts or gets angry, the person ceases to be rational and will end up making more mistakes and omitting important things that could have been communicated properly and understood if the person's emotions were under control.

This Woman made a choice to be clothed with strength and dignity. As women, how can we be clothed with strength? The Bible tells us in Nehemiah 8:10c, "Do not grieve, for the joy of the Lord is your strength". So, in this scripture, the joy of the Lord strengthens. For us to wear on strength, we need joy. Even on cloudy days and seasons where she would rather prefer to stay in bed or just run very far away and stay alone, she wakes up each morning and gets dressed up in the joy of the Lord. You can't tell what she's been through by her appearance, whether it's a good day or bad day, because all you will see is the joy of the Lord that she radiates. As virtuous women, we refuse to wear the labels people put on us or the situations we have been through. We refuse to wear labels of bitterness, anger, envy, jealousy, gossip, wrath, lies and deception. We refuse to wear labels of hate, frustration, stress, depression, worry and anxiety. We refuse to accept the status quo. From today, we are deliberate on what we choose to be clothed with and by our confession we choose strength and the joy of the Lord.

Finally, one of the synonyms of the word, "strength" is stability. This means to be stable, to have balance (balance of mind), mental health, and soundness. The bible says, "For God has not given us the spirit of fear, but of power, and of love, and of a sound mind" (2 Timothy 1:7). God has given us the spirit that keeps our mind stable. Don't ever entertain negative thoughts. Your mental health is very important. Most times our hearts deceive us. In Jeremiah 17:9, "the heart is deceitful above all things and desperately wicked: who can know it". I remember the days when my heart will tell me lies about my husband and why he acted in a certain way towards me or tell me that people are thinking in a particular way (negative thoughts) towards me and I would believe it and start acting based on what my heart tells me. The idea was to fight the peace of my mind and cause me to lose my mind

> **We refuse to wear labels of hate, frustration, stress, worry and anxiety. We refuse to accept the status quo.**

or become someone who isn't nice. Rather than listening to your heart, listen to God. He wants to clothe you with a sound mind.

The bible instructs us in Philippians 4:8 MSG, "Summing it all up, friends, I'd say you'll do best by filling your minds and meditating on things true, noble, reputable, authentic, compelling, gracious—*the best, not the worst; the beautiful, not the ugly;* things to praise, not things to curse". Think pure thoughts! Think noble thoughts! Think lovely thoughts! Think godly thoughts! As much as you may want to think lightly of this, the bible further tells us how we can achieve this in Proverbs 4:23 which says, "Above all else, *guard your heart,* for everything you do flows from it". It is our responsibility to have "monitoring equipment" for our hearts. Monitor per second, per minute, per hour and so on, of everything that goes in and out of your heart. Once it won't give God glory, once it isn't pure, noble, honest, reputable, lovely etcetera, discard it immediately.

According to Lexico, the word honour means "high respect; great esteem".

Declare After Me:

- I take back my dignity
- I take back my self esteem
- I take back my self-worth
- I take back my self-respect
- I take back my self confidence
- I walk away from my past. My past is behind and buried and it will stay buried forever in the name of Jesus.

- Today, I open a new chapter of my life; and in this new chapter, I am clothed in strength and dignity.
- No one will take advantage of me because I am a woman or because I am naïve and innocent.
- From henceforth, I will make wise decisions.
- I possess the right attitude, mindset, and qualities that will attract accolades to my life and all those connected to me in Jesus' name.
- O Lord, I will not be afraid of the future. Every spirit of fear, I command you to get out of my life now in the name of Jesus.
- O Lord, the Bible says in Job 3:25, "What I feared has come upon me; what I dreaded has happened to me". So I decree and declare that I will not give fear power over me again. I will never allow fear grip me. I am an overcomer in the name of Jesus.
- Today I decree over every challenge, or problem in my marriage, business, career, relationship, health, finance, I command you to disappear. I live above every challenge or problem in the name of Jesus. Amen!!!
- I Will Always Laugh Without Fear Of The Future. I Declare, My Future Is Bright; My Future Is Great! My Future Is Secure In The Name Of Jesus.
- I am a strong woman.
- I am clothed with strength.
- I reject frustration, tiredness, lack, depression, loneliness, and emptiness.
- I will not be weighed down.
- I am unstoppable. No one and nothing will slow me down.

- I have the mind of God.
- I am clothed with a sound mind.
- My emotions are stable; I refuse to be emotionally unstable.
- I walk in the wisdom of God.
- I have a discerning spirit.
- My spirit man is alert and sensitive in Jesus name, Amen.

ACTIVITIES

DAY 1

#CHALLENGE 9: *"Strength and honour are her clothing; and she shall rejoice in time to come" (Proverbs 31:25 KJV).*

ACTIVITY 1: Get rid of every garment of frustration, bitterness, anger, tiredness, emptiness, loneliness and put on the garment of a quiet and calm spirit. The bible says, "I can do all things through Christ which strengthens me" (Philippians 4:13); that is who you are.

- Don't compare yourself with others. Your work and journey with God is personal to you.

ACTIVITY 2: Choose to be joyful throughout today whether you feel like it or not. Your happiness or joy shouldn't be tied to your environment. If your environment or the people around you make you happy, good! However, if your environment and the people in it are the ones that want you to be unhappy, reject it and choose to be happy and stay happy. Joy isn't tied to the way people treat or don't treat us. It comes from within. It comes from an understanding of who we are in God. It comes from a personal walk with God.

List the things you need to do to stay joyful:

_____

_____

_____

_____

_____

- We are not the products of our emotions. Your emotion doesn't have the power to keep you down unless you give it the power.
- You are in control of your emotions.

ACTIVITY 3: Discard self-pity. It robs you of your happiness and joy. Your situation isn't the worst; the lie of the enemy is to make you believe that your case is so bad. Be glad and rejoice!!! Happiness is a choice while joy comes from within and it is lasting.

DAY 2

#CHALLENGE 9: *"Strength and honour are her clothing; and she shall rejoice in time to come" (Proverbs 31:25 KJV).*

ACTIVITY 1: Evaluate your thoughts; is your mind sound?
- Find out what triggered the thought.
- Determine how to silence strange voices or any voice that isn't the voice of God.

ACTIVITY 2: Ask and answer these questions for yourself:
- How do I dress? Modestly or immodestly?
- How do people perceive me? (good girl/woman or bad girl/woman)
- What is my disposition to infidelity?
- How do I treat my spouse? Respectfully or Disrespectfully?
- Who is the head of my home? Me or My Husband
- Are you faithful to your spouse (Yes or No)

- For the Singles, are you faithful in your relationships (Yes or No)
- Do you gossip? (Yes or No)
- Are you lazy or hardworking (Yes or No)

If your answers were more negatives than positives and you are the head of your home and not your husband, you need to intentionally work on yourself so as to make the necessary changes of becoming the woman God called you to be.

DAY 3

#CHALLENGE 9: *"Strength and honour are her clothing; and she shall rejoice in time to come" (Proverbs 31:25 KJV).*

ACTIVITY 1: Write down or make a list of what makes you scared about the future? It could be your marriage, career, business, finance, relationships, health, academics, etcetera.

_____

_____

_____

ACTIVITY 2: Pray against every spirit of fear.
- Father today I break every bondage of fear operating in my life in the name of Jesus.
- I decree just as the bible says perfect love casts out fear, today I receive the love of Jesus and I hereby declare, the fear of tomorrow is destroyed in the name of Jesus.
- Today I decree that I walk and live in love, peace and a sound mind in the name of Jesus.

Chapter

11

CAREER

FINANCE

LIFESTYLE

MINISTRY

FAMILY

GIFTED

#CHALLENGE 9: *"Strength and honour are her clothing;*
and she shall rejoice in time to come"
(Proverbs 31:25 KJV).

*O*ur new challenge introduces an interesting quality possessed by the Proverbs 31 Woman. This woman was a clothier as well as a couturier. This is because in Proverbs 31:24, we read that she designs gowns and sells them, and brings sweaters she knits to the dress shops. Her ability to make her own clothing means that she was able to manage her resources well. We also see that she was good at what she did. The bible says in Proverbs 31:22 that everything she wears is beautiful. For the Proverbs 31 Woman in contemporary times, you may not be a couturier; however that's a good skill to acquire; but what strikes me from this scripture is the excellence portrayed in her work.

It becomes expedient that whatever we are doing, we should always do it well. The bible says in Ecclesiastes 9:10, "Whatsoever thy hand findeth to do, do it with thy might; for there is no work, nor device, nor knowledge, nor wisdom, in the grave, whither thou goest".

Whatsoever career path or course of life you have chosen in business, or academics, be known for doing your best. Be known as outstanding. Be known as an expert in the area you choose. Never underestimate or place little attention or value to the place of preparation. Keep building capacity, and keep improving on yourself.

One of the reasons why I believe this woman was able to manage her resources is because she could cut the cost of sewing clothes through clothiers. So, you can imagine how she would have successfully reduced the amount of money she spent on looking good. As virtuous women, you need to look good obviously, but you need to find ways to achieve this at minimal cost. You shouldn't spend most of your earnings on clothes, shoes, and material items just because you need to look good. There's a lot you need to do with your money. There are several investments to make, people you need to help and be channels of blessings to, charitable works to undertake, seeds and offerings to give to God and your family members. So, money is needed for other matters beyond just your looks.

There are several investments to make, people you need to help and be channels of blessings to, charitable works...

For the Proverbs 31 Woman, she made her own clothes; so, for those who are designers, great! Some may literally learn how to sew or look for other ways to minimize spending. She wasn't a woman that bought clothes on credit; so, we need to count the cost first, save up for the things we need and buy them when we can afford it. Never feel pressured to look good or to dress well because the people you are trying to impress really do not care.

Don't be in debt in order to live up to a false life or sponsor a false lifestyle. You aren't in competition with anyone. There's so much falsehood in our society today. Some people are driving cars they can't afford, living in houses they can't pay for and have a standard of life that they can't sustain. Don't make your life about impressing people. The truth is that no one really cares.

Be real. Be true to yourself. Be authentic. Be a person of integrity. Imagine if you are trying to impress someone by living beyond your means and the person you are trying to impress is doing the same? I believe there will be a time that you will be able to fund whatever lifestyle you desire under God, but wait for the time. For those who can fund such lifestyles, celebrate them and step aside while waiting for your own time. Eccl. 3:1 says, "There is a time for everything, and a season for every activity under the heavens:" Don't measure the distance or type of your destiny's journey or assignment with another man's own. Your assignment is unique to you.

The bible says in 1 John 2:16 (NLT) that "For the world offers only a craving for physical pleasure, a craving for everything we see, and pride in our achievements and possessions. These are not from the Father but are from this world." I like the way it's said in Contemporary English Version "our desire to have *everything* we *see*". Our desire to have everything we see most times causes us to live fake lives. We must be careful as women in these contemporary times not to fall into the trap of the enemy, by being ruled by the lust of the flesh and the pride of life.

> **Don't make your life about impressing people. The truth is that no one really cares.**

The Proverbs 31 Woman as seen in this verse understands what it means to live within her budget. I love the fact that it is very possible to get the things you need at very affordable prices depending on where you go to shop. Not every kind of market or store is yours. So, find yours and stick with it and still look good and classy. Some bible translations say that she dresses in colourful linens and silks. Colours when worn properly with consideration to matching colours or skin tones and the season of the year (optional) are beautiful to behold. When you dress colourfully, the colours make you radiate, glow and even look lively. The Proverbs 31 Woman in the bible radiated beauty and warmth. It was definitely beyond just looking good, but I believe her dresses created a lively,

The Proverbs 31 Woman in the bible radiated beauty and warmth. It was definitely beyond just looking good...

friendly and fascinating atmosphere wherever she went to. Like the Proverb that says we are addressed the way we are dressed, I believe she had a lot of kind remarks and gestures because of how she dressed.

Be very intentional!!! Be very deliberate!!!

The Proverbs 31 Woman in our contemporary times is a woman that carries an aura of joy, cheerfulness, gentleness, kindness and is good natured. For anyone to possess these qualities, that person must feel good within herself. You can't fake joy, cheerfulness, or kindness; it comes from within. Every woman must be in control of her emotions. You must intentionally choose to be joyful every new day and stay joyful throughout the day. Your feelings shouldn't be a product of your environment, but rather the state of your heart. Even when people do things to you that should make you upset, intentionally refuse to let their actions or inactions affect the state of your heart. I know you may be saying it's difficult, I agree but that's the way God wants us to be. When we say we are becoming more like Him or that we were created in His image and likeness, it means that we are in control of our environment. God gave us dominion over everything. Your disposition is very important. You don't need to feel good to dress good. Always dress good and your feelings will fall in line. Even when you don't feel good, act like you are good and eventually your feelings will begin to align.

PRAYER FOCUS

The Proverbs 31 Woman is a gifted woman. She is the kind of woman everyone will love to be around.

- O Lord, *please cause me to be gifted. Teach me all I need to know.*
- O Lord, *May I never be my own limitation in life in the name of Jesus.*
- O Lord, *show me how I can impact those around me with my lifestyle in the name of Jesus.*
- O Lord, *cause me never to get tired of doing good, of building my capacity and staying relevant. May my generation be blessed because of me in the name of Jesus.*
- O Lord, *fill my heart with joy, peace and love in Jesus' name.*

AMEN!!!!

ACTIVITIES

DAY 1

#CHALLENGE 10: *"She does her own sewing, and everything she wears is beautiful" (Proverbs 31:22 CEV).*

ACTIVITY 1: You will be answering these questions:

1. Are you industrious?

2. How does your family perceive you? (hardworking, lazy, laid back)

3. What skills do you possess that can generate funds?

If there is nothing you do currently, please find a skill, learn and gain mastery in it. However, if you are already skilled in some things, make sure you are constantly improving yourself and staying updated in your area of specialization.

_____

_____

_____

_____

_____

_____

_____

_____

_____

DAY 2

#CHALLENGE 10: *"She does her own sewing, and everything she wears is beautiful" (Proverbs 31:22 CEV).*

ACTIVITY 1: Be very deliberate with what you wear. Dress in colourful linens, silks and cottons.

- If you love just dark colours, it's time to spice up your wardrobe with some bright, warm colours.

ACTIVITY 2: Make someone else happy today. Help someone face their own challenging situation.

- How many people did you make happy today or make feel good about themselves?

_____

_____

_____

_____

- Pray for someone who is going through a tough time now. Take a deliberate step by being good to someone today.

_____

_____

_____

_____

_____

_____

DAY 3

#CHALLENGE 10: *"She does her own sewing, and everything she wears is beautiful" (Proverbs 31:22 CEV).*

ACTIVITY 1: Our Activity for today is *very **prophetic***. You will sing songs of joy or prophetically speak joy into every situation and circumstance that wants you to stay sad, bitter, angry, depressed, etcetera. Just keep singing or declaring it until you begin to feel light and joyful.

Scripture Focus:
Nehemiah 8:10, "Nehemiah said, "Go and enjoy choice food and sweet drinks, and send some to those who have nothing prepared. This day is holy to our Lord. Do not grieve, for the joy of the Lord is your strength."

Romans 14:17, "For the kingdom of God is not a matter of eating and drinking, but of righteousness, peace and joy in Holy Ghost.

Today is not for grieving rather it's a day of joy.

ACTIVITY 2: Be deliberate in creating a striking impression today. Look good; act and feel good.
- Step out in joy.
- Be free to enjoy your womanhood.
- Deliberately breathe in and breathe out and enjoy yourself while you do so.
- Give yourself a treat (you don't need anyone to do that for you); Go for a spa, massage, facials, and just pamper yourself!

- Wear a nice fragrance and dress up for you and not because you want to impress someone.
- Sing out loud; raise your voice and worship God. Add a dance to it.

  Smile more.

ACTIVITY 3: Do whatever you know will make you happy and is God approved.

- If you are physically tired and exhausted, try soaking your body in a warm bath for some minutes and just relax. You can add a nice relaxing music at the background.
- You can tap yourself on your shoulder; appreciate yourself. It's okay to encourage yourself.
- We all have different ways of unwinding, so whatever works for you, do it. Don't wait for people to treat you right; rather treat yourself and the people around you right.

This isn't a license for us to become lazy or selfish; rather, this is to help us build inner strength to move ahead. Always know that the odds are not against you. God is always and will forever be with you.

Stay Strong! Stay Winning! Continue to give your best in that relationship! It won't be long, and you will smile again!

_____

_____

_____

_____

DAY 4

#CHALLENGE 10: *"She does her own sewing, and everything she wears is beautiful" (Proverbs 31:22 CEV).*

Your personal hygiene is very important in becoming a Virtuous Woman.

Remember To:
- Bath at least twice a day.
- Use deodorants, body sprays/splash and perfumes.
- Wash your under wears properly and ensure they are always clean before you wear them.
- Wash your hair regularly, especially for those who sweat a lot.
- Don't wear a wig/weave-on or braids for a long time without washing your hair intermittently.
- Brush regularly, floss and use mouth fresheners.
- Shave or take off the hairs in your armpit and private part regularly.
- Avoid wearing damp clothes or clothes that aren't properly dried.
- Dress decently.
- Dress up and look good.

You can achieve all these on a low budget.

Chapter

12

CAREER

FINANCE

LIFESTYLE

MINISTRY

FAMILY

BALANCE

#CHALLENGE 11: *"She designs gowns and sells them,
brings sweaters she knits to the dress shops"*
(Proverbs 31:24 MSG).

*E*arlier, we read in Proverbs 31:16 that with the money she's put aside, she plants a vineyard meaning that she was a vineyard owner and most likely in the wine business. Then by Proverbs 31:24, we read that this woman was the Chief Executive Officer of a manufacturing outfit. The King James Version of the Bible says she sells to merchants. A merchant is a person or company involved in wholesale trade, especially one dealing with foreign countries or supplying goods to a particular trade. This "Wonder" woman (*I call her*) is totally worthy of emulation.

For the Proverbs 31 Woman to successfully sell in bulk, she probably had many people working for her because wholesalers buy in bulk. So, she must have had enough for bulk sales to her clients. How was this woman able to handle the pressure that comes with owning multiple businesses, being a wife and a mother all at the same time and nothing suffered? I believe she modeled the virtues in Galatians 5:22 (NLT), "But the Holy Spirit produces this kind of fruit in our lives: love, joy, peace, patience, kindness, goodness, faithfulness, gentleness, and self-control. There is no law against these things! When you receive the Holy Spirit into your life, you will produce these different fruits which will be made manifest by your lifestyle, and as such, you will be able to bear any situation and handle pressure calmly. This woman as seen from the book of Proverbs is one woman who understood how to successfully balance her life, thus, no area of her life suffered a mishap or shipwreck.

In today's society, we have many women who have tried to be virtuous but haven't gotten it right in the area of creating balance. Some areas of their lives do well while some other areas suffer and often times, the home front gets affected the most. Some women have had to give up their marriages in order to pursue their career. What makes the Proverbs 31 Woman different is that she doesn't have to give up any part of her life. She has it all. Balance is important for the 21st Century Woman on the journey to becoming a Proverbs 31 Woman. We must have a work-life balance as virtuous women in the 21st Century. As you pursue your ambitions, dreams and aspirations, you can also have a balanced life. It is possible.

Balance is important for the 21st Century Woman on the journey to becoming a Proverbs 31 Woman.

One of the ways this Woman was able to create balance was by making productive use of her time. She understood the value of time and never wasted it on unproductive ventures or associations. We were told of the different areas of her life, but I noticed there was no mention of her social life. The Bible didn't tell us how many friends she had and her relationship with them or tell us of her extended family. I believe she must have had friends that sparked the creative juices in her and not friends that would have discouraged her from dreaming big. As we strive to become this Woman in contemporary times, the association you keep is very important. If you are going to become this Woman, you must have friends or a network of like minds that will help you become the kind of woman you see in your dreams.

These are the kind of people you need to surround yourself with:
- Dreamers
- Dream enablers
- Dream interpreters
- Encouragers

In other words, you need motivators around you and not what I call, "fire extinguishers". There are people who if they are in your company, for every beautiful idea or dream you have, they will always have a way of downplaying it and ultimately causing you to lose zeal towards it. For some of us, our biggest challenge right now is that we do not have time. When you begin to understand that you do not have the time, your time will be more productive, and you will have better outcomes and results. Proverbs 16:27 (TLB) says, "Idle hands are the devil's workshop; idle lips are his mouthpiece". I usually read this scripture in the past and stopped at idle hands, but the bible also talks about idle lips as the devil's mouthpiece. When you aren't busy you become a vessel to work and speak the mind of the devil. You become his staff and work under his employment.

Today I want to encourage you, even if you think you are busy, you can get busier. There's so much more to do and we have little time to achieve all of it on earth. Jesus said in John 9:4 (NIV) "As long as it is day, we must do the works of him who sent me. Night is coming, when no one can work". A time is coming when you won't be able to drive that car, learn that skill, start that business, get that job, ride that bicycle, walk for a long distance, shout and jump even when you feel like. The night seasons will meet each of us at some point in our lives so, just like Jesus, we must do the works of Him who sent us while it is still day. This scripture in Psalms 90:12 (NIV), "Teach us to number our days, that we may gain a heart of wisdom", is another reminder of how we should put our time to productive use. Simply put, if we learn how to number our days, we will grow in wisdom.

Hard work doesn't kill anyone; rather, it pays to be hard working.

There are people still putting in more hours and effort than you are to their work and life. They work harder than you to ensure that no part of their lives collapses. Hard work doesn't kill anyone; rather, it pays to be hard working. Work with your hands and your head. Gone are the days of sitting at home and doing nothing; you can sit at home (take care of your children) and still own a business or even businesses. You can stay at home looking after your children and still be the think tank for your family. You can stay at home and have capital investments. Just make sure that whatever course of life you take, you aren't wasting your own time.

Don't be comfortable and satisfied depending completely on others to meet your needs. You can be the one meeting the needs of others by virtue of your financial standing. Don't be comfortable with no ambition. Stretch your mind. You are God's masterpiece. He put so much in you for you to be satisfied with living a mediocre life. There are territories to take, cities and nations to possess. All you need to be that woman is already in you. There are seeds God has deposited in you and it's time to nurture them. It's time for them to bear fruit. Grow it.

Declare After Me: I believe I can be more!!! There's room for more.

PRAYER FOCUS

Dear Virtuous Woman, in the book of Proverbs 31:24, we read that this Woman designs gowns and sells them. To design is to create. We are like our Father in heaven. We were created in His image and likeness. The Bible tells us that God created the heavens and the earth in six days and on the seventh day He rested. If we are like God, then as women we have the power and ability to create things out of nothing and use it for profitable purposes. Today, you will cry out to God to make you creative and to fill your heart with fresh ideas.

- O Lord, *stir up every creative ability in me. Today I decree, any creative ability in me, begin to manifest now in the name of Jesus.*
- *Today, I receive fresh ideas for my business, career, marriage, relationships, academics, etcetera.*
- *Today, I receive the power to create and make wealth in the name of Jesus. For the Bible says in Deuteronomy 8:18, "But thou shalt*

PRAYER FOCUS

remember the Lord thy God: for it is He that giveth thee power to get wealth, that He may establish His covenant which He swore unto thy fathers, as it is this day."

- O Lord, *please grant me my own cutting edge. Help me to carve a niche for myself in the name of Jesus.*

- O Lord, *I receive fresh ideas that will distinguish me in the name of Jesus.*

- O Lord, *with all you will be doing for me in my new season, please help me to stay humble in the name of Jesus. I will not become arrogant or disrespectful towards my husband or the people around me, in the name of Jesus.*

- O Lord, *make me a blessing to my family and my generation in the name of Jesus.*

Amen! Amen! Amen!!!

ACTIVITIES

DAY 1

#CHALLENGE 11: *"She designs gowns and sells them, brings sweaters she knits to the dress shops"* (Proverbs 31:24 MSG).

ACTIVITY 1: Look through all the busyness around you and ask yourself if you are getting "productive" results at the end of the day.

_____
_____
_____
_____

- For some of us, we may need to drop some of the things that take our time and pick up new activities, jobs, businesses, or hobbies that are more productive or value driven.

ACTIVITY 2: Discover new ways of doing more and being more.

_____
_____
_____
_____

- That business that has been in your heart, it's time to go out there and do it. Don't entertain fear. You can also own businesses. If this woman could be all of these when there wasn't technology, I believe we are of a more privileged generation and should do better.

DAY 2

#CHALLENGE 11: *"She designs gowns and sells them, brings sweaters she knits to the dress shops" (Proverbs 31:24 MSG).*

ACTIVITY 1: How can you turn your hobby to a business opportunity? What do you need to put in place in other to generate wealth from that thing you love to do?

_____

_____

_____

_____

ACTIVITY 2: Pray for discernment and for divine direction.

- O Lord, *please show me how to make wealth from the things around me.*
- O Lord, *please show me that one thing I am good at doing. Please show me that one thing or things that I love to do and teach me how to earn a living from them.*
- O Lord, *I declare that the gifts and talents you have placed in me will not remain or stay dormant. I will put them to use starting from today.*
- *The Bible says the gift of a man makes room for him. O Lord, please cause my gift(s) to make room for me in Jesus' name.*
- *Today, I decree and declare, I am a wise woman. I am hard working. I am industrious. I am financially stable. I earn a living and I use it to support my family and for kingdom assignments in the name of Jesus.*

Amen!!!!

DAY 3

#CHALLENGE 11: *"She designs gowns and sells them, brings sweaters she knits to the dress shops" (Proverbs 31:24 MSG).*

ACTIVITY 1: For starters, begin with your immediate environment. Proffer solutions to your immediate environment by meeting a need.

ACTIVITY 2: Those already in business, plan on how you can reach a wider customer base. How can you expand what you are currently doing to reach more people?

ACTIVITY 3: Pray for God's grace and favour. You need the help of the Holy Spirit. The bible says that Jesus found grace and favour with God.

- Pray about your ideas and ask for divine direction. Also ask God when to move or expand. Don't do it alone.
- Seek counsel.

_____
_____
_____
_____
_____
_____

DAY 4

#CHALLENGE 11: *"She designs gowns and sells them, brings sweaters she knits to the dress shops" (Proverbs 31:24 MSG).*

ACTIVITY 1: Monitor and keep a close watch on everything that goes on in your home.

- Keep an eye on who you leave your children with irrespective of the sex of the care giver. Your child may be passing through an abuse that you aren't even aware of. When they aren't expecting you to show up or enter the room, just show up and see what is going on.

- Ask God for the spirit of discernment to know what is going on around you, especially in your home. You may really be amazed at what you will discover.

- Most especially, depending on what you discover, ask God for wisdom to handle the information. There is a way that seemeth right to a man, but the end is destruction (Proverbs 14:12). God needs to guide you and help you. Seek good counsel.

DAY 5

#CHALLENGE 11: *"She designs gowns and sells them, brings sweaters she knits to the dress shops" (Proverbs 31:24 MSG).*

ACTIVITY 1: Ensure that rules are obeyed by those who live with you.

- Please note, I didn't say shout at them nor did I say abuse people in the process. Remember, in one of our earlier challenges, the virtuous woman always speaks kindly. Speaking kindly should become your default setting.

ACTIVITY 2: Ensure that in your absence (like when you go to work), your domestic staff and children are adhering to all the laid down instructions at home.

- Finally, in all that we do, let's hand over the running of our homes and the safety of our homes to God. No one can keep it better than God. I pray that God will keep our homes safe from harm and accidents in the name of Jesus.

Amen!!!

_____

_____

_____

_____

_____

_____

Chapter

13

CAREER

FINANCE

LIFESTYLE

MINISTRY

FAMILY

INSPIRATION

"She keeps am eye on everyone in her household
and keeps them all busy and productive"
(Proverbs 31:27 MSG).

I personally love the way the Message translation of the Bible puts it, "she keeps an eye on everyone in her household". It just shows you that though she is a very busy woman and may go out in the morning and return in the evening, yet she knows everything going on in her home. Some women in the 21st Century who have a 9:00am to 5:00pm kind of job have lost touch with what happens in their homes. For some who work in the banks, it's even more of an emergency. Some women have abandoned consciously or unconsciously, the running of their home to nannies, relatives and even strangers. You aren't aware of what your children have been exposed to in school and even at home by the so-called nannies and relatives taking care of them. Some children are going through verbal, mental or physical abuse by the same people supposed to take care of them and you may be unaware. Some mothers don't know the friends of their children, or if your child is being bullied in school or at home. You are completely ignorant of some of the challenges your children are going through. Even the people you have trusted with your home may be stealing from you or cheating you, and yet you are unaware. This woman in the bible could categorically state the position of things in her home, how her children were doing, and what her servants do while she is at home, or away. She was completely in charge of both the physical and spiritual atmosphere of her home ensuring that everyone did what they were supposed to do, and at the right time.

> **She was completely in charge of both the physical and spiritual atmosphere of her home...**

Everyone at her home was under her watchful eyes. She knew when they were sick and when they needed care. She knew where her provisions and food items where kept; she knew who came to her house. She was the one in charge of assigning duties to everyone ensuring that no one was idle or lazy. In contemporary times, the likely things that could happen from not keeping an eye on all that goes on in our homes are stealing, wastage, an untidy home, lack of discipline and control, children being endangered, abused or molested, adultery/fornication, dishonesty amongst those living with us, children picking up bad habits, behaviours, addictions, etcetera. There are always consequences for every action. If we do not take our place in our homes, somebody else may do so or things may generally suffer and spoil. We need to take ownership of the daily running of our homes and stop making the excuse that we are too busy. Whatever you value, you prioritize. Our homes should be one of our priorities. There's no one that will run your home better than you.

The Proverbs 31 woman should be a huge inspiration and motivation for all women. The Bible says she carefully watches everything in her household, meaning that she pays great attention to everything happening at home to avoid problems or accidents. It also shows that she is in charge and in control of her home. She is the land lady of her home. When we are in charge, we can manage our resources effectively, we ensure that there are no wastages; we ensure that accidents are avoided and the people that live with us are responsible and accountable. We take responsibility for how things turn out in our homes because we shape them by our actions.

Chapter

14

CAREER

FINANCE

LIFESTYLE

MINISTRY

FAMILY

CONCLUSION

We have come to the end of the Proverbs 31 Woman Challenge, but this isn't the end of the journey of becoming who God has called us to be. I tried giving you the tools you need to successfully build your character, personality, marriage, home, career and business without anyone of them suffering or failing. The Proverbs 31 Woman was a woman who was able to combine and effectively manage every area of her life and succeeded in doing that as well. One thing is very important for the 21st Century Woman and it is "balance". We need to aspire and achieve building a life of balance.

I know we belong to a dispensation that isn't willing and ready to pay the price for success. We belong to a selfish generation, but we learnt that this Woman was selfless in all her dealings. We can be selfless in all our dealings – marriage, relationships, etcetera.

You can do this. We are even in a better dispensation than the Proverbs 31 Woman was in. We are in the dispensation of grace. The grace of God makes everything easy. Ask God to help you become a Virtuous Woman. I join my faith with yours and I decree it is done in Jesus' name. Amen!

In Proverbs 31: 29-31 the bible says, *"Many women have done wonderful things, but you've outclassed them all! Charm can mislead and beauty soon fades. The woman to be admired and praised is the woman who lives in the Fear-of-God. Give her everything she deserves! Festoon her life with praises!" (Proverbs 31:29-31 MSG).*

This Woman was praised because of her love and fear of God. Charm misleads and blinds the admirer while our beauty diminishes as we grow older, but one thing that will abide and stand the test of time is our character, which is who we are in our relationship with man and God. This wouldn't fade. Our focus as women should always be to keep growing spiritually. Our walk with God and love for God should never be compromised.

The Proverbs 31 Woman was placed on a class of her own. She was highly distinguished for who she was. This is a call to women to sit up and take your place. Don't ever believe the lie that you can't be anything or nothing good can come out of you. Don't let culture or status quo keep you in a box. You can be more, and you can achieve more. My prayer for every married woman today is that your home will be filled with laughter, joy, dancing and singing in the name of Jesus. Whatever has stolen the peace, love, joy, and laughter from your home, ends today in the name of Jesus. I pray that you will never meet a future full of disappointment and that every strong challenge affecting the peace of your home ends today in the name of Jesus.

For the singles, I pray for you today, you will not marry a wicked man. Your husband wouldn't have extramarital affairs. I pray that both you and your spouse will love Jesus and your eyes will be single (focused on Jesus). I pray that joy and laughter will never depart from your homes. I pray that you will be a Virtuous Woman and that your children and husband will praise you. I pray from the depths of my heart: may you have a good life. The longer it lasts, the better and sweeter it will get. May you and the husband of your youth age gracefully together in the name of Jesus. Amen!

Finally, my prayer to every woman and man who reads this book is that you will fulfill purpose. You will leave the earth empty. You will make huge impact and be a generational force to reckon with in Jesus' name. I pray your love for God will never wane; rather, as each day ends and another starts, so will your hunger, passion and fire for God rise in Jesus' name.

Amen!!!

Personal notes

_____
_____
_____
_____
_____
_____
_____
_____
_____
_____
_____
_____
_____
_____
_____
_____
_____
_____
_____
_____
_____
_____
_____
_____

Personal notes

Personal notes

_____
_____
_____
_____
_____
_____
_____
_____
_____
_____
_____
_____
_____
_____
_____
_____
_____
_____
_____
_____
_____

Personal notes

_____
_____
_____
_____
_____
_____
_____
_____
_____
_____
_____
_____
_____
_____
_____
_____
_____
_____
_____
_____
_____
_____
_____

Best Selling Author of

I ALMOST RUINED MY MARRIAGE

My true life story!

My journey in the early years of marriage was quite painful and enduring. Nothing I knew seemed to make sense anymore. All the seemingly harmless habits I got away with in the course of my life as a single became a challenge in marriage.

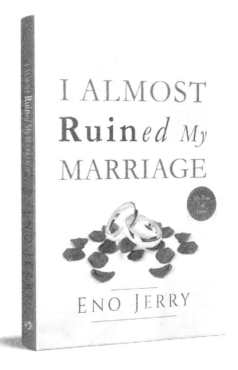

When you marry a near-perfect man like I did, your flaws become so glaring. The sad truth is that before I got married, I never considered these habits as flaws. Have you ever found yourself saying things like: "This is how I have always been and people accepted and liked me"? Have you also found yourself saying to your spouse, "Hey, you met me like this; why is this now a big deal"? Oh, I said this a thousand and one times. I just couldn't understand how anyone will want me to change. Who I was had taken me so many years to become, so why was I supposed to change just because I got married. Hmmm, that was a difficult one for me to crack.

In this book, I will be sharing my journey so far, what I had to learn in the process and who I have become through my experiences.